This forking book
belongs to:

_____

Welcome!
Everything is fine.

Forking Good

An Unofficial Cookbook for Fans of *The Good Place*

Written by Valya Dudycz Lupescu and Stephen H. Segal

Illustrated by Dingding Hu

QUIRK BOOKS
PHILADELPHIA

Library of Congress Cataloging in Publication Number: 2019930331

ISBN: 978-1-68369-155-6

Printed in China

Typeset in Brandon Grotesque and Proforma

Designed by Elissa Flanigan
Illustrations by Dingding Hu
Production management by John J. McGurk

Quirk Books
215 Church Street
Philadelphia, PA 19106
quirkbooks.com

10 9 8 7 6 5 4 3 2 1

This cookbook is dedicated to our beloved ancestors,
who have inspired our hearts and minds and pots and pens
with good food and thoughtful conversation

We hope they are in the Good Place

Contents

—————

"When I'm really upset, concentrating on a table of contents helps me calm down. It's like a menu, but the food is words."

—Chidi, Season 2, Episode 5, "The Trolley Problem"

MORAL DESSERTS

WHERE EVERY JANET KNOWS YOUR NAME

Introduction

Why is there so much food, and talk of food, in *The Good Place*—a supernatural TV sitcom that's all about learning to use ethical philosophy to make good life choices? From the first moments of the first episode, food forms the backdrop to almost everything that happens on the show.

We meet Eleanor Shellstrop as she wakes in the afterlife and immediately learns that she died while buying groceries. Then Michael, her angelically dressed soul shepherd, takes her on an orientation tour of the Good Place, and literally the first thing we see as they stroll onto the neighborhood's streets is a cupcake cart.

Food puns fill the Good Place's ever-changing neighborhood signage. And once Eleanor meets her new friends Chidi, Tahani, and Jason, they quickly fall into a casual routine of noshing at parties and restaurants, chatting in sidewalk cafés, and not-so-silently judging one another for their food choices, from Jason's adolescent snack cravings and Tahani's Instagram-perfect hors d'oeuvres to Chidi's unnecessary muffin dilemmas and Eleanor's knee-jerk shrimp-and-booze gluttony.

After a while, it becomes clear that food in *The Good Place* is a kind of emotional litmus test for what's happening all around.

In the beginning, food underscores the uncanny, nearly-perfect-but-still-somehow-unsatisfying quality of life in the neighborhood that Michael has designed. (Frozen yogurt in every flavor you never imagined!) Three seasons of mind-blowing plot twists and reinventions later, food continues to reflect the nature of the characters' surroundings. (A horrifying pot of chili representing Nietzsche's idea that life is meaningless!)

Food, it turns out, is fundamentally a philosophical subject.

Philosophy encourages us to take a step back and reflect upon our choices. This approach can be applied to food as well, because the way a person cooks—and eats—reveals something about the way they have chosen to live their life.

How many meals do we eat that are fine but unremarkable, that fill the void but leave something to be desired? Do we eat without thinking about where the food comes from or how it was made? Do we invite our neighbors for a barbecue or host a potluck for friends? Do we ask elders for their favorite recipes, maybe adapt them for our needs but celebrate the legacy? Do we take time to enjoy the process of putting new things together? Do we take creative culinary risks in order to learn, to grow—to become better?

We wanted to write a cookbook inspired by *The Good Place* because *we* were inspired by *The Good Place*. In a show that explores the meaning of life, food is a way to highlight values.

The Good Place's creator, Michael Schur, brilliantly creates a vivid world and lovable, flawed characters. This cookbook is our love letter to the show—to food, to puns, and to philosophy. You can make these recipes for yourself or your family to accompany your next binge-watching session, or you can scale up for a viewing party with friends. These dishes were created with sharing in mind.

The Good Place loves its characters, and so we grew to care about them too. Through all of their mad adventures, we cheer them on to become better people. Along the way, their story inspires us to think about how we, too, can become better people.

Our hope with this cookbook is that after being inspired by *The Good Place*, maybe people will take a little time out to think about the role of food in their lives. After all, recipes are a lot like philosophical theories. Both are guidelines for how to do something that's central to living.

Perhaps a little thoughtful reflection and some new dishes can do for us what philosophy and friendship did for Eleanor, Chidi, Tahani, Jason, Michael, and Janet.

Maybe thinking about the way we eat can actually change our lives.

We invite you to join us now as we try to cook our way into the Good Place.

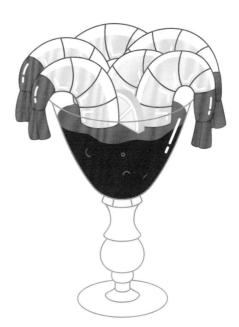

Valya's Pantry: Not a Void

The all-knowing afterlife-support assistant named Janet is able to conjure anything that the residents of the Good Place want, whether that means a plate of jalapeño poppers, a couples therapy session, or a never-ending shrimp dispensary. Where does it all come from?

Janet, and by extension her infinite void, manifests everything she and the others need. It's not really a void, after all. As she puts it, it's a "subdimension outside of space and time at the nexus of consciousness and matter tethered to my essence." Janet's void is not unlike Doctor Who's TARDIS or Mary Poppins's carpet bag: it's where she keeps the magic.

Janet's omnipotence in conjuring would be an amazing power to have for cooking. We can at least have the next best thing: a well-stocked pantry. Once we take the time to fill up the cupboards with the right staples for our individual needs, our ability to whip out just what we need can seem like magic, too.

My barometer for a well-stocked pantry is one that allows me to cook something healthy and delicious for my family even when I haven't gone grocery shopping for a few days. With one teen on a gluten-free diet, and another who is a picky eater, it's not always easy coming up with ideas. But necessity is the mother of invention, and my years of practicing the spontaneous manifestation of mealtime means that this cookbook is full of options for an array of palates and dietary needs.

When I moved into my current apartment, I replaced the door to my pantry with one that has paneled glass windows. Some people think that's odd, but food is beautiful: baskets of onions and potatoes; glass jars filled with nuts, seeds, and other treats; canisters of flours and pastas; herbs and spices and oils and sauces. It makes me happy to see all the ingredients when I'm walking through the kitchen. It helps me visualize the possibilities.

What follows is a list of most of the basic ingredients you'll need to cook the recipes in this cookbook. You'll notice that in addition to gluten-free options, I tend to cook with a lot of peppers and spices—I like to think of them as bringing out the bright, hot heart of a dish. I also love different types of salts and use them to punctuate natural flavors. You don't need to amass a collection, but I would recommend taking the time to taste the differences if you have a spice shop nearby. (At least begin with coarse and fine kosher sea salt in your pantry, for flavor and crunch.)

Of course, there are many things in my pantry not included here—a greater variety of beans and nuts and flours, for example. I try to keep many of the less-perishable items on hand, and I buy fresh whenever possible.

In Plato's *Protagoras*, Socrates tells Hippocrates: "Knowledge is the food of the soul." It's not a coincidence that I think of pantries in much the same way I think of bookcases. Both are places where we go to be nourished and sometimes find the inspiration to start something new . . . and hopefully forking good.

Basics

- Aromatics: Garlic, ginger
- Bread crumbs (regular or gluten free)
- Oils: All recipes that call for olive oil refer to extra-virgin olive oil. For recipes that require oils with higher smoking points, I recommend grapeseed oil, avocado oil, walnut oil, and coconut oil.
- Vinegars: Apple cider vinegar, balsamic vinegar, red wine vinegar, white wine vinegar, and unseasoned rice vinegar
- Salts: Most recipes call for kosher sea salt but I also recommend Maldon salt, pink Himalayan salt, black and red Hawaiian salt, and smoked salt.
- Spices: Black peppercorns for freshly ground pepper, berbere, ground cayenne pepper, celery salt, chili powder, ground cinnamon, crushed red pepper, ground cumin, curry powder (sweet and Vindaloo), mustard powder, ground nutmeg, nutritional yeast flakes, Old Bay seasoning blend, paprika (sweet and smoked), poppy seeds, sesame seeds, dried thyme, ground turmeric
- Tomato paste

Baking

- Dry ingredients: Baking soda, baking powder, cornstarch, cream of tartar, unsweetened cocoa powder
- Extracts: Vanilla, lemon
- Flours: All-purpose, whole wheat, gluten-free blend (can substitute one-for-one with regular flours), corn (masa harina), tapioca flour, almond flour
- Sugars and sweeteners: Granulated sugar, dark brown sugar, light brown sugar, powdered sugar, honey, maple syrup

Pantry staples

- Canned goods: Black beans, fire-roasted tomatoes, hominy
- Capers
- Chicken broth
- Chiles: Chipotles in adobo, pickled jalapeños
- Gingersnaps and graham crackers
- Medjool dates
- Nuts: Raw and roasted cashews, pecans, hazelnuts, walnuts
- Roasted red peppers
- Plums in syrup
- Salsa

Condiments and sauces

NOTE: *some of these are refrigerated.*

- Creamy horseradish
- Liquid smoke
- Soy sauce
- Sriracha
- Stone-ground mustard
- Tahini
- Toasted sesame oil
- Worcestershire sauce
- Tamari

Equipment

- Bamboo skewers (4- or 6-inch)
- Toothpicks

Dairy and eggs

- Butter: Recipes that call for butter generally refer to salted butter, although a few require unsalted butter.
- Cheeses: Cheddar, chihuahua, Danish blue, goat cheese, havarti, manchego, mozzarella, parmesan, swiss
- Eggs: Recipes that call for eggs refer to large eggs. For baked goods, room-temperature eggs make a world of difference.
- Milks: Almond milk, buttermilk, cashew milk, heavy whipping cream, whole milk
- Other: Greek yogurt, mayonnaise, and sour cream (full-fat versions are best but you can adjust to your dietary preferences)

Produce

- Fresh herbs: Dill, mint, parsley
- Citrus: Lemons, limes, navel oranges for juicing and zesting
- Onions: Yellow, white, shallots
- Peppers: Jalapeño, red bell pepper, yellow bell pepper

---- DIETARY KEY ----

Throughout the book, you'll see icons that indicate recipes
that can be tailored to specific dietary preferences.

GF = gluten free option   **V** = vegetarian option   **VG** = vegan option

Reboot
the Day

Hume Fries

"I read this entire Hume book, and then I read it again because I didn't understand it the first time, and now I'm ready to go."

—Eleanor, Season 1, Episode 4, "Jason Mendoza"

In Season 1, Chidi begins Eleanor's afterlife ethics lessons with what he thinks will be a simple assignment: reading David Hume's *A Treatise of Human Nature*. The text is widely considered one of the most influential works in the history of philosophy, and in it Hume presents the idea that what we think of as an individual is a collection of perceptions that change with time and with encounters with other people. Hume breaks down the concept of personality into thought, action, and relationships. Each of those perceptions, he points out, influence the others.

Eleanor quickly bores of talking about Hume and suggests that she and Chidi get to know her neighbor Jianyu. Chidi misunderstands—he thinks she has connected Hume to Jianyu's selfless Buddhism and is trying to learn from the virtuous monk's good influence. Not so much; she just wants to escape the lesson.

It's hard to fault any new student for resisting an introduction to Hume. If our existence is a collection of moments that we experience with our senses, process with our minds, and can recall in our memories . . . where is the self in that? If those feelings and perceptions are all we have, then each of us is nothing but a bundle of perceptions that change over time. That's tough to swallow.

HUME AND BEING

"I may venture to affirm of the rest of mankind, that they are nothing but a bundle or collection of different perceptions, which succeed each other with an inconceivable rapidity, and are in a perpetual flux and movement."

—David Hume, "Of Personal Identity," from *A Treatise of Human Nature*, 1739

Being: I'm not a bundle of anything. I'm me! I'm different from everyone else.

Hume: How do you know?

Being: Everybody's different. We make different choices, we do different things.

Hume: Exactly. Let's try it with fries. What is a french fry?

Being: A potato. A vegetable.

Hume: Right, but it's not the same as a baked potato or mashed potatoes.

Being: Nope. It's cut into slices or wedges and fried. Sometimes it's topped with cheese. Or chili. Or gravy and cheese curds. Ooh.

Hume: So what makes a french fry different from fried zucchini or fried cauliflower?

Being: It's totally different! It's crispy on the outside, soft on the inside, smells kinda nutty and deliciously greasy, is a little bit crispy, and is always perfectly salted.

Hume: You described what it looks like, tastes like, feels like, and smells like, but what *is* it?

Being: But that's what it is. I can only describe what I experience.

Hume: Exactly. *That's* bundle theory.

Our hybrid recipe for oven-baked home fries, which have the look and shape of french fries, is named in honor of Hume. This three-potato medley emphasizes the "bundling" of different components to create something unique and special. The Moroccan-inspired seasonings are a departure from the usual American breakfast fare. Just as Eleanor adds a new set of experiences and relationships to reshape her personality in the afterlife, we introduce new ingredients to a familiar dish to reshape our perceptions of what it means to be a fry.

Hume Fries

V GF

SERVES: 6

1 lb sweet potatoes

½ lb yellow potatoes

½ lb purple potatoes or russet potatoes

4 tbsp vegetable oil or coconut oil

½ tsp ground cumin

1 tsp ground cinnamon

1 tbsp ground turmeric

½ tsp ground cayenne pepper

1 tsp paprika (either sweet or smoky)

2 tbsp honey

Kosher salt to taste

Freshly ground black pepper to taste

2 tbsp fresh mint or cilantro, minced

- Preheat the oven to 400 degrees Fahrenheit. Line two baking sheets with parchment paper.
- Cut all the potatoes lengthwise into ¼-inch slices and then cut slices into ¼-inch strips.
- In a large bowl combine the oil, spices, honey, and salt and pepper to taste. Add yellow and purple potatoes and toss to coat. Use a slotted spoon to transfer potatoes to one of the prepared baking sheets, reserving the oil mixture. Bake for 10 minutes.
- While the potatoes are cooking, toss the sweet potatoes in the oil mixture. Transfer to the second baking sheet.
- After the first pan has baked for 10 minutes, place sweet potatoes in the oven. Bake both pans for 40 to 45 minutes, tossing every 15 minutes.
- Remove pans from oven, transfer potatoes to a large bowl, and fold in mint. Serve warm.

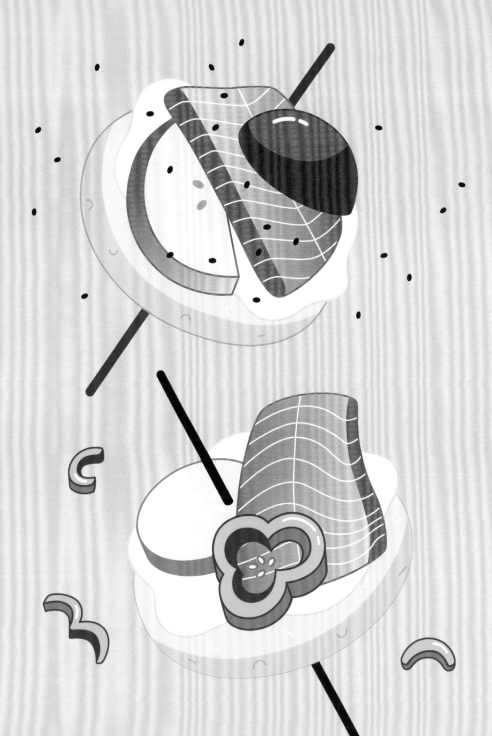

Hegels and Lockes
(Brunch on a Stick)

Chidi: "No way! Soul mates are real?"
Michael: "They sure are. Although your soul mate situation is a little unusual."
Chidi: "Oh, no! I don't have one, do I? That's fine, I mean, who
needs a soul mate, anyway? My soul mate will be . . . books!"

—Season 2, Episode 1, "Everything Is Great"

Some things complement each other so well that they seem made for each other, even when they appear to be opposites: peanut butter and jelly, macaroni and cheese, pork chops and applesauce, hot pretzels and mustard, chocolate and strawberries, bagels and lox, Bert and Ernie, Abbott and Costello, Batman and Robin . . . and Eleanor and Chidi?

The interesting thing about these supposed perfect soul mates who turned out to be no such thing is that their partnership nonetheless often worked—sometimes as friends, sometimes as lovers. Even when Michael switched their circumstances, they still found ways to love and improve. This seems to suggest that in the Good Place, soul mates are more about finding the right person at the right time rather than about tapping into any metaphysical matchmaking mojo.

That "love the one you're with" epiphany holds true for the show's friendships and creative partnerships, too. It's hard to imagine that Tahani and Eleanor would have been pals (or soul mates, for that matter) during their time on Earth, but in many reboots in the Good Place they form genuine bonds.

This brings us to two philosophers separated by time and space: Georg Wilhelm Friedrich Hegel and John Locke.

Locke, known as the "Father of Liberalism," was a seventeenth-century English philosopher who believed that governments should be democratic, tolerate religious difference, and uphold human rights. Locke criticized the idea that people have innate ideas about the world, arguing instead that we must gain knowledge through our senses and reasoning.

Meanwhile Hegel, born a century and a half after Locke, is considered to be the most important philosopher of the idealist school of German rationalist philosophy. He was basically a personal, political, and philosophical authoritarian who despised the democratic idea and spirit. For Hegel, the state is the embodiment of the "world soul," and the best rulers would be a group of philosophers just like him, with the ability to deal with the "true interests" of humanity.

PHILOSOPHICAL ODD COUPLE?

Hegel and Locke are opposites in many of their ideas. Even if they had lived in the same time and place, it seems unlikely that the men would have been friends. Or would they?

Both were born after the last known person was let into the Good Place, so we can hypothesize that the two men *could* have met in the Bad Place after their deaths, where they might have discussed their opposing philosophical systems while being tortured. In the metaphysical petri dish of the afterlife, maybe they even forged the kind of affection discovered by Chidi and Jason and the rest of Team Cockroach?

We like to imagine them in a kind of philosophical Odd Couple scenario: Hegel as the neurotic, organized, and domineering neat freak; and Locke as his fun-loving, creative, and messy roommate.

For this dish, we took inspiration from the many "on a stick" restaurants and kiosks seen in *The Good Place*. The pun-filled second episode of Season 2 included Steak on a Stick, Caviar on a Stick, Hot Dog on a Stick on a Stick, and Bagel on a Stick. We've deconstructed the classic bagels and lox brunch and present our special Good Place version, with Locke's lemon honey cream cheese and Hegel's horseradish dill spread. Presented together—each on a stick, both on a platter—we think they complement each other well.

Hegels and Lockes

SERVES: 6–10

3 bagels, the best locally made ones you can find

8 oz cream cheese, divided

1 tbsp poppy seeds

1 tbsp sesame seeds

1 tbsp honey

1 tsp lemon juice

1 tsp lemon zest

½ Granny Smith apple, cored and cut into 1-inch squares

8 oz smoked salmon, sliced into 2-inch strips

12 cherry or grape tomatoes, halved

1½ tbsp finely minced shallot

1 tsp chopped fresh dill

1 tsp store-bought creamy horseradish

3 Persian cucumbers, sliced

1 yellow bell pepper, cut into 1-inch pieces

- Halve bagels, toast, and cut each half into eighths to create 48 bagel bites. Set aside.
- Divide the cream cheese in half. Place each portion in a small bowl.
- In another small bowl combine poppy seeds and sesame seeds. Set aside.

For Locke's Lemon Honey Cream Cheese:

- Mix honey, lemon juice, and zest into one bowl of the cream cheese until incorporated. Generously spread mixture on 24 bagel bites.
- To assemble: Slide one bagel bite onto a toothpick, followed by one piece of apple, a slice of salmon (folded or cut to fit the bagel bite), one piece of tomato, and a sprinkle of poppy seed–sesame seed mixture.

For Hegel's Horseradish Dill Cream Cheese:

- Mix shallot, dill, and horseradish into the other bowl of cream cheese until incorporated. Generously spread mixture on the remaining 24 bagel bites.
- To assemble: Slide one bagel bite onto a toothpick, followed by one piece of cucumber, a slice of salmon (folded or cut to fit the bagel bite), and a piece of yellow pepper.
- Arrange on a serving platter.

Nietzsche Lorraine

"We're trapped in a warped version of Nietzsche's eternal recurrence!"

—Chidi, Season 2, Episode 2 "Dance Dance Resolution"

The philosopher Friedrich Nietzsche believed human beings are "surrounded by a fearful void"—an image familiar to *Good Place* fans, though Nietzsche's idea of a void is very different from Janet's infinite void of existential quantum storage ("a subdimension outside of space and time at the nexus of consciousness and matter, tethered to my essence," as she defines it).

Nietzsche thought humans live in a horrible, meaningless universe where life is suffering and all we can do is try to find meaning in it. He was obsessed with the idea that, given infinite time and a finite number of events, those events will continue to happen again and again, forever. Which sounds a little like Michael's neighborhood reboots in Season 2. Though 802 is not an infinite number, it's a lot. And when Chidi and Eleanor finally learn the truth of all those reboots from Mindy St. Claire in the Medium Place, Chidi is inclined to despair. However, they don't give up. They return to the neighborhood to try to find a solution once again.

Nietzsche's answer was to love the present moment, in acceptance of the fact that we'll relive it over and over. But his solution doesn't quite apply to what the Soul Squad deals with. Rather than forcing them to experience the same events repeatedly, Michael wants to achieve a *different* outcome, so he designs each reboot with crazier and crazier variables: different soul mate configurations, best-person awards, fields of cacti, pig farms, giant bugs, and plenty of new pun-derful restaurants.

In honor of those restaurants and of variations on a good thing, we present you with: Nietzsche Lorraine.

A GOOD PLACE MASTERQUICHE

The origin of quiche, like the origin of Nietzsche, is German. The word *quiche* comes from the German word for cake, *Kuchen*, and it was created in the medieval kingdom of Lothringen, later renamed Lorraine by the French.

The dish began as a typical German egg custard pie and got its name from the baked bread crust, which was more like a brioche bread roll than the pastry crust commonly used today. Like Michael's subtle, or not-so-subtle, variations of the neighborhood, quiche lorraine can be prepared many different ways: often (but not always) with swiss cheese, sometimes with onions in the Alsatian style, and stuffed with salmon, spinach, broccoli, or other tasty fillings.

This recipe is a new take on the old, crusty favorite. We've removed the crust altogether (because let's face it, we're not really sure what the foundation of *anything* in the Good Place actually is) and we've added potatoes, in the style of tortilla española.

We think it's much more delicious than a clam chowder fountain and almost as clever as a ponzu scheme.

NOTE: *This recipe takes time. It's not one of those eight-second butt reboots, but it's totally worth it.*

Nietzsche Lorraine

SERVES: 8–10

5 or 6 Yukon gold potatoes, peeled

1 cup olive oil, divided

1 yellow onion, diced

¾ tsp kosher salt, plus more to taste

6 large eggs

8 slices Canadian bacon, cooked according to package directions and cut into ½-inch slices

6 oz swiss cheese, shredded

- Preheat oven to 450 degrees Fahrenheit.
- Halve potatoes lengthwise, then slice approximately ⅛ inch thick. Set aside.
- In a large ovenproof nonstick or cast-iron skillet over medium-high heat, heat ⅓ cup of the olive oil. Add onion and ¼ teaspoon of the salt; cook, stirring occasionally, until softened and starting to caramelize, about 10 minutes. Transfer onions to a large bowl and set aside.
- Add another ⅓ cup olive oil to the same pan and return to medium-high heat. Add potato slices and salt. Sauté for 1 minute. Reduce heat to low and cover, stirring occasionally, until potatoes are tender and lightly browned in places, about 20 minutes.
- Transfer the potatoes to the bowl with the onions, leaving the remaining oil in the pan. Let potatoes and onions cool slightly.
- In a small bowl, beat the eggs well; add salt to taste. Add eggs to the cooled vegetables. (If the vegetables are still warm, the eggs will scramble.) Mix gently with a wooden spoon, taking care not to break the potatoes. Gently fold in Canadian bacon. Let stand for 5 minutes.
- Add the remaining ⅓ cup olive oil to the skillet with the oil from the potatoes and place over medium-high heat. Add the egg mixture and cook for about 2 minutes, using a rubber spatula to carefully loosen mixture from the sides of the pan to help it spread evenly.
- Reduce heat to medium-low. Cook the quiche, continually loosening the sides to allow any uncooked egg to run off the top of the quiche and make contact with the pan, for approximately 15 minutes.
- Transfer the skillet to the oven. Cook for 4 to 5 minutes, until the top of the quiche is firm, with no apparent wetness.
- Remove from oven and top with swiss cheese. Turn on the broiler, return skillet to oven, and cook for 2 to 3 minutes, until cheese is melted and lightly browned.

Shake the pan gently to make sure the entire quiche has fully set. It should be firm without any wobbling.

- Remove the skillet from the oven and cover it with a large ovenproof plate. Carefully flip over the pan and plate at once and slide the quiche onto the plate.

- Slice quiche into thin wedges and serve immediately, or let cool to room temperature before slicing and serving. Quiche can also be refrigerated and then served either cold or slightly warmed.

Eggsistential Crisis

"Searching for meaning is philosophical suicide. How does anyone do anything when you understand the fleeting nature of existence?"

—Michael, Season 2, Episode 4, "Existential Crisis"

A n existential crisis usually occurs at that significant moment when one thing ends and another thing begins. In the case of the characters on *The Good Place*, this happens to be the juncture between life and the afterlife. For the still living, it can occur when one changes jobs, relationships, or living situations, or when one moves into a new phase of life. An existential crisis prompts an individual to ask themselves: What's next? Where do I go from here?

Each main character in *The Good Place* has an existential crisis at some point during their afterlife adventures that leads them to question the meaning of life. Even Michael, afterlife architect extraordinaire charged with fashioning fresh ways to stimulate humans through eternity, experiences an emotional breakdown about whether or not his "life" has value or purpose.

Though he didn't use the term *existential*, Søren Kierkegaard is generally regarded as the father of existentialism. Much of his writing deals with the necessity of grappling with anxiety as a way of living an authentic life. Kierkegaard went as far as to suggest that anxiety is necessary for creativity because anxiety is produced by the overwhelming freedom of possibility. Choosing an option among a myriad of possibilities is part of life—and the foundation of great art.

When Chidi starts trying to teach Michael how to be a good "person" in Season 2, he tells his fellow dead human friends: "I have to force him to think about what we used to think about: that life has an end, and therefore our actions have meaning." When Michael rejects his simplistic immortal perspective, he faces many new possibilities of who he can be now. What will he do? What will give his life purpose?

Artists, writers, and philosophers have been searching for ways to answer these questions of existential meaning for hundreds of years: Friedrich Nietzsche, Albert Camus, Jean-Paul Sartre, Simone de Beauvoir, Fyodor Dostoyevsky, Martin Heidegger, Franz Kafka, Ralph Ellison, Jean-Luc Godard, Richard Wright, Ingmar Bergman, Stanley Kubrick, and many others. From theater to television sitcoms, the concept of the existential crisis reaches into our lives, our afterlives, and now into our kitchens . . .

THE MEANING OF . . . EGGS?

Eggman: You have before you a dozen eggs packed in their carton, untouched. What will you do with them?

Walrus: What can I do? What ingredients do I have?

Eggman: You have access to any ingredients you need.

Walrus: I could . . . make an omelet? Or a few omelets?

Eggman: That's certainly an option.

Walrus: Wait, but is it the *best* option? Is this a test? What is the best use of my time? I can make eggs benedict, or blueberry muffins, or a frittata . . . or I could hard-boil them and make deviled eggs, or crack them raw into a protein smoothie. Would that be healthier? Maybe I should give them away? What does it say about me if I eat them all myself? Should I have a party and invite people over? Make an egg hunt? Become vegan? Argh! It's all too much! There are too many options! I don't know which one is the best! I . . . don't . . . know . . . what . . . to . . . do!

Versatile and delicious, eggs can be prepared and served in a myriad of dishes, baked in quiches, scrambled with cheese, folded into cakes and muffins, poached, fried, whipped—the list goes on and on. There are so many possibilities that the options *can* seem overwhelming. How can you pick just one? Which one is the best? After all, potential and freedom are at the heart of so many existential crises . . . and eggsistential ones as well.

In many ways, eggs are an excellent symbol for the potential of an authentic life. They've been a symbol of life and rebirth for thousands of years across many cultures, a perfect metaphor for the Soul Squad, whose death and rebirth (undeath? Redeath?) are integral to their growth and reflection.

Michael dealt with his existential crisis by dabbling in the tropes of a human male midlife crisis: a youthful haircut, a sportscar, an earring, a tattoo, speaking in slang, and samba lessons. None of these responses satisfy because they're short-term, instant-gratification distractions. They avoid the reality that a breakdown of identity isn't the time to be someone else; it's the time to cultivate an authentic self.

Eggsistential Crisis

V **GF**

SERVES: 8–10

2 tbsp olive oil

½ large onion, diced

2 garlic cloves, minced

1 red bell pepper, seeded and diced

1 yellow bell pepper, seeded and diced

1 4-oz can green chilies, diced

1 15-oz can diced fire-roasted tomatoes

1 tsp chili powder

½ tsp ground cumin

1¼ cups canned black beans, drained and rinsed

Kosher salt to taste

Freshly ground black pepper to taste

10 large eggs

½ cup all-purpose or gluten-free flour

1 tsp baking powder

½ cup (1 stick) salted butter, melted and cooled, plus more for greasing casserole dish

8 oz cheddar cheese, shredded

- Preheat oven to 375 degrees Fahrenheit. Butter a 13-by-9-inch casserole dish.
- In a frying pan over medium heat, heat olive oil. Add onions, garlic, and peppers and sauté until vegtables are soft and onions are translucent, roughly 10 minutes.
- Add chilies, tomatoes, chili powder, and cumin. Lower heat to medium-low and cook for 5 minutes.
- Stir in black beans. Add salt and pepper to taste. Remove from heat.
- Crack eggs into a large bowl and beat with a hand mixer, electric mixer, or whisk. In another bowl, combine flour, baking powder, and a dash of salt. Slowly pour flour mixture into egg mixture, and stir with a spoon until fully incorporated. Add cooled melted butter, bean mixture, and cheese. Mix well.
- Pour mixture into the prepared casserole dish. Bake for 45 minutes until golden-brown and firm on top.
- Let cool for 10 minutes. Slice into large squares and serve.

Add Hominy

"Ya basic."

—Eleanor

Sometimes persuasive arguments have so much passion behind them that they successfully influence an audience—and yet they are logically flawed. When an argument fails to support its claim with reason, we call that a fallacy. Many kinds of fallacies exist, but identifying one can be tricky. Aristotle set out to do so in his work *On Sophistical Refutations*, in which he looked critically at arguments and where they go wrong.

One of the most common fallacies is the ad hominem fallacy. It occurs when, instead of attacking the points of someone's argument, you attack the person making the argument. For example, one could make the following arguments about the Soul Squad:

- "Tahani says the humans deserve a second chance, but she's an elitist who thinks she deserves everything good, so she can't be taken seriously."
- "Jason is a fan of the Jacksonville Jaguars, and they suck, so he doesn't know anything."

Focusing on the character's personality is completely irrelevant to each argument. A wide variety of traits and observations can constitute an ad hominem attack, and many stem from prejudicial stereotypes (such as those about debutantes and Jaguars fans).

In Season 2, Episode 11, the humans arrive at the all-knowing and all-seeing Judge Gen's chambers, where they plan to make their cases for why they should be allowed into the Good Place. But they're never allowed to present those arguments, flawed with fallacies or not, because Judge Gen "absorbs the entirety of [their] existences," which allows her to understand exactly who they are—and whether or not they *really* belong in the Good Place. There's no hiding behind ad hominem fallacies with an omniscient authority like Judge Gen, who is so attuned to what motivates humans that she uses their emotions to flavor her burritos. Of envy, she says, "It's really good on Mexican food. It gives it a little kick."

We added our own little kick to our hominy recipe in the form of green chilies, which serves as a reminder that ad hominem fallacies always add a bit of fire to an argument.

Add Hominy

SERVES: 8–10

16 oz sliced bacon

1 small onion, diced

2 garlic cloves, minced

1 jalapeño, seeded and diced

1 4-oz can green chilies, diced

2 15.5-oz cans hominy, drained and rinsed

1 tsp smoked paprika

½ tsp ground turmeric

Kosher salt to taste

Freshly ground black pepper to taste

½ cup shredded chihuahua or cheddar cheese

- Preheat oven to 350 degrees Fahrenheit.
- In a skillet over medium heat cook bacon until crispy. Cool, crumble into a bowl, and set aside.
- Pour off all but 2 tablespoons of bacon drippings from the pan. Add onions and garlic and sauté over medium heat until onions are soft and translucent, about 10 minutes. Add jalapeño and chilies. Cook for another 5 minutes.
- Add hominy, paprika, and turmeric. Cook until hominy is lightly browned, about 10 minutes. Add salt and pepper to taste.
- Add about two-thirds of the crumbled bacon and stir to combine. Pour hominy into a casserole dish. Bake for 15 minutes.
- Sprinkle cheese on top of the hominy and bake for an additional 5 to 10 minutes, until cheese is bubbling.
- Sprinkle the remaining crumbled bacon over the casserole and serve hot.

I Kant Believe It's Not Buttermilk Pancakes

"In this realm, IHOP stands for Interdimensional Hole of Pancakes. You don't really eat these pancakes. It's more like they eat you."

—Michael, Season 2, Episode 10, "Rhonda, Diana, Jake, and Trent"

When Chidi agrees to teach Eleanor about ethics, he turns to Immanuel Kant's *The Groundwork of the Metaphysics of Morals*. In it, Kant creates a basis for defining what behaviors are ethically acceptable (and, further, what behaviors are ethically required). Kant believed that ethical action was guided by the so-called categorical imperative of rules that produce ethical behavior if they are followed. It was his opinion that immorality is the result of a person holding others to a different standard of behavior than they do for themselves.

In Season 2, Episode 10, Chidi struggles against the obvious need to lie to maintain the Soul Squad's aliases when they find themselves in the Bad Place. He tells Eleanor that according to Kant, lying is always wrong. He tells her, "Principles aren't principles when you pick and choose when you're gonna follow them!" Eleanor declares herself a moral particularist, invoking the philosopher Jonathan Dancy to make the argument that, "You have to choose your actions based on the particular situation." Eleanor wins that round, and the conflicted Chidi tries to blend in.

The limitations of Kant's categorical imperative don't seem to apply in the absurdity of the afterlife. Kant may have argued that the contradiction of standards was immoral, but what happens when you have a completely different set of rules to follow, because you're literally in hell? Or when you find yourself at . . .

THE INTERDIMENSIONAL HOLE OF PANCAKES

In Season 3, the Soul Squad arrives in the Neutral Zone between Good and Bad, at the Interdimensional Hole of Pancakes—the crossroads of all dimensions, where the pancakes contain interdimensional portals and want to eat *you* as much as you want to eat them. The Judge augments reality to make this place appear as a regular IHOP, but dangers still exist. As Michael warns the humans, "If you eat anything in this IHOP, you will literally explode." Chidi missteps and falls into a portal, shrinks, and tumbles through time and space. Before he's retrieved, he gets a glimpse of the Time Knife, which he describes as "a trillion different realities folding onto each other like thin sheets of metal, forming a single blade."

For the indecisive deontological philosopher who spent his life in perpetual conflict for being unable to make the simplest of decisions, what does it mean to see so many dimensional possibilities at once? We're not sure; he seems to snap back into their dimension fairly easily. Fortunately, the glimpse of the fractalesque reality did not launch him into the existential crisis that Jeremy Bearimy did.

So how does this influence *our* pancake recipe?

Some version of it has been part of the human diet for thousands of years, so it's fitting that the crossroads of all dimensions is a symbolic house of pancakes. The earliest written reference to a pancake is the *tagenia* from ancient Greece, mentioned in the writing of the fifth century B.C.E. poets Cratinus and Magnes, and made with flour, olive oil, honey, and milk.

There are versions of pan cakes all over the world: Ethiopian injera and Indonesian serabi, French crêpes and German Pfannkuchen, Chinese bing and Indian cheela—some sweet, some savory, all grain based. In America, the earliest pancakes were likely made with cornmeal or buckwheat and called flapjacks or johnnycakes. Buttermilk pancakes, which are perhaps the most popular iteration in the United States, are believed to have come from Scotland, where they are called drop scones and made with a leavening agent that produces a taller cake than the typical crêpe-like British pancake.

Our vegan version drops the buttermilk and eggs but still captures the delicious fluff and flavor. And they won't try to eat you.

I Kant Believe It's Not Buttermilk Pancakes (VG)

MAKES: 25–30 silver dollar pancakes

1 cup all-purpose flour

2 tbsp baking powder

½ tsp kosher salt

2 tbsp coconut oil, melted and cooled slightly (use refined for a neutral flavor or unrefined if you want a stronger coconut taste)

1 cup vanilla almond milk

¼ cup maple syrup

Vegetable oil or coconut oil to grease the griddle/pan

Powdered sugar and fresh fruit, for topping

- Preheat the oven to 200 degrees Fahrenheit. Line a baking sheet with parchment paper. Set aside.
- In a small bowl, combine flour, baking powder, and salt. In a large bowl, combine melted coconut oil, milk, and syrup.
- Add dry ingredients to the wet, stirring until just incorporated. Don't overbeat the batter or the pancakes will be tough.
- Allow batter to sit for 5 minutes while you heat a griddle or a cast-iron skillet on medium-low heat. The pan is ready when a drop of water sizzles upon contact.
- Lightly grease the griddle with vegetable oil or coconut oil.
- Using a large spoon, ladle small portions, about a heaping tablespoon, of batter onto the griddle. (You want the pancakes to be bite-sized.)
- When bubbles form in the batter, use a spatula to flip pancake and cook for another minute or two. Transfer cooked pancakes to the prepared baking sheet and warm in the oven while you cook the remaining batter.
- Sprinkle with powdered sugar and top with the fruit of your choice.

Flake Flortles

"Want some breakfast? I know how to make cereal."

—Jason, Season 2, Episode 5, "Existential Crisis"

Through eight hundred reboots, second chances, void rebirths, and eternal judgment, few things have remained unchanged for *The Good Place*'s four humans and their otherworldly companions. The only constant in all of the timelines might be Jason Mendoza's love affair with the Jacksonville Jaguars and, specifically, their quarterback, Blake Bortles. Jason's undying devotion permeates all the dimensions: from his dapper Bad Place alias Jake Jortles to his habit of shouting "Bortles!" every time he launches a Molotov cocktail (which he does surprisingly often). His loyalty is total and unwavering.

TILL DEATH DO THEY MEET

When we consider the morally questionable lives our four human protagonists led before they died and awoke in Michael's neighborhood, a question arises: was loyalty a virtue they ever displayed?

Eleanor: Too self-absorbed and too afraid of being hurt to get close to people, her only loyalty was to herself.

Chidi: Too indecisive and paralyzed to act, any shred of loyalty he possessed was torn apart every time he had to make a decision.

Tahani: Concerned only with the way that other people, especially her parents, perceived her value, she displayed on-the-surface loyalty to anyone who increased her supposed worth.

Jason: For all his flaws and ignorance, he genuinely cared about people. He was fiercely loyal to Donkey Doug and Pillboi, devoted to the members of his dance crew, and committed to the Jacksonville Jaguars. It might have led him to make some bad decisions, but Jason's loyalty was never in question.

Michael: Initially he is loyal to his torture experiment. Soon his loyalty extends to include Janet as he begins to care about her and doesn't want to keep "killing" her with each reboot. In time, he comes to care about the humans and their growth and redemption.

Janet: Not a girl, and not a robot, at first Janet doesn't have the ability to feel loyalty. Each time Michael kills her and she reboots, Janet evolves and begins to develop feelings. She also becomes loyal to Michael and the humans, especially Jason, with whom she has her most complicated and emotional relationship.

In his book *The Philosophy of Loyalty*, American philosopher Josiah Royce defines loyalty as the "willing and practical and thoroughgoing devotion of a person to a cause." When a group of people have a shared cause, he says, that cause develops moral significance. We see this happen as Eleanor, Chidi, Tahani, and Jason open up to one another. Eventually, they become a community committed to a shared purpose, and their loyalty ultimately spreads to include Michael and Janet.

Where *does* loyalty fall in their ethical exploration? Season 1 focuses on the shared cause of learning how to be better people to earn their place in the afterlife. Season 2 is devoted to proving they *are* better people than they were when they died. Season 3 asks whether they might have been better people on Earth if they'd had one another's support down there. Each time, their community of four (and eventually six) bonds and they become even more fiercely devoted to one another.

Flake Flortles pays tribute to that loyalty. Cereal may be simple and easy. It might not be fancy, like eggs benedict, or Instagram worthy, like a luscious stack of pancakes. But it's sweet and delicious and gets the job done—just like Jason. And even though people underestimate cereal, it might turn out to be the secret ingredient that holds everything together.

Flake Flortles

V

SERVES: 8–10

6 cups sweetened corn flake cereal

½ cup unsweetened flaked coconut

1 tsp ground cinnamon

Pinch of ground nutmeg

6 large eggs

1 cup milk

1 tsp vanilla extract

12 slices bread

Butter or oil for frying

Honey or maple syrup for drizzling

- Preheat the oven to 200 degrees Fahrenheit. Line two large baking sheets with parchment paper.
- Place cereal in a large plastic zip-top bag, press out all the air, and seal tightly. With a rolling pin or your hands gently crush cereal into tiny pieces.
- Pour cereal into a large bowl. Mix in coconut, cinnamon, and nutmeg. Transfer approximately one-fourth of this mixture into a smaller, shallow bowl. This will be the dipping bowl.
- In another bowl, whisk together eggs, milk, and vanilla.
- Cut each slice of bread into four triangles. Set aside on a large plate.
- Heat a griddle or nonstick frying pan on medium-low heat. Grease well with butter or oil.
- Dip each piece of bread into the egg mixture, fully saturating both sides. Let the excess drip off, then dip into the smaller bowl of crushed cereal to coat on both sides. You may want to press the cereal gently into the bread to make sure it sticks.
- Return prepared french toast triangles to the plate. As you work, refill the smaller bowl as needed and discard any cereal that gets too wet or sticky.
- Working in batches, fry the triangles for 2 to 3 minutes per side. When done, transfer to the prepared baking sheets and place in the oven to keep warm.
- Serve with honey or maple syrup.

Chaos and
Hors d'Oeuvres

Cod Is Dead

"You put the Peeps in the chili pot and eat them both up! You put the Peeps in the chili pot and add the M&Ms! You put the Peeps in the chili pot and it makes it taste bad!"

—Chidi, Season 3, Episode 4, "Jeremy Bearimy"

In **Season 3, Episode 4,** after Chidi learns the truth about the Brainy Bunch's near-death experiences, their afterlife adventures, and the universe's quantification of goodness, Michael explains that time not only isn't a straight line, it's in fact shaped like the phrase "Jeremy Bearimy" written in cursive. "This broke me," Chidi says, speaking to everyone and no one. "I—I'm done."

He spirals into an existential crisis that culminates in a nihilistic classroom rant to his students as he stands over a pot of noxious chili made from canned meat and bags of candy. Along the way to that final meltdown, he pauses briefly to quote Friedrich Nietzsche to a hapless drug dealer:

"God is dead. God remains dead. And we have killed him. Who will wipe this blood off us? What festivals of atonement, what sacred games shall we need to invent?"

Nietzsche wrote these words in *The Parable of the Madman* in response to the timely idea that if people no longer needed God to provide moral guidance, and if governments no longer needed the legitimacy of divine right, then the human-invented idea of God had essentially been destroyed by scientific thought. Nietzsche worried that this conclusion would leave humanity hopeless and pessimistic. His antidote was for each person to cultivate their own meaning of life. In his 1889 book *Twilight of the Idols*, Nietzsche wrote, "He who has a why to live for can bear with almost any how."

Having had his understanding of the universe yanked out from under his feet, Chidi abruptly loses his "why." That's why he starts adding nonsensical ingredients to his chili. That pot of insanity makes as much sense to him as the whole of existence does.

After processing their fate, the soul mates, led by Eleanor and accompanied by their otherworldly guides, come to a similar conclusion to Nietzsche's. It's also the conclusion the Austrian psychiatrist and Holocaust survivor Viktor Frankl reached in his quest to understand what sustained his fellow survivors and gave purpose to their lives, as well as the lives of all people. The answer was searching for a way to live a life of meaning, through work, love, or a sense of purpose.

There is sense to be made of the world—we just have to make it ourselves. Life choices, like chili peppers, need to be applied with careful consideration.

What gives a chili pepper purpose? Using it to its full potential in a recipe, of course.

———————

The chili pepper provides heat and flavor; it is the bright, hot, heart of any dish.

Consider fish tacos. They have their roots in coastal areas of Mexico where people have been wrapping seasoned fish in corn tortillas for centuries. In the past fifty years or so, a prototypical Baja California version of the dish has become popular: tortillas stuffed with battered and fried white fish, such as cod, topped with cabbage, lime, and a mayonnaise-based sauce. Such tacos are delicious but not dogma. At fish stands all along the West Coast, many inspired variations are served. The cod is dead, but what we do with it is ultimately a personal choice.

Fish tacos are tasty, but the kick of the chipotle pepper makes them transcendent. Chili peppers have been consumed in Mexico for thousands of years; the word *chili* has its roots in the Nahuatl language of the Aztec people. So the question is not whether or not we need some chili pepper in our recipe, but rather: how much? In matters of food and faith, the answer comes down to an individual experience of the divine.

Cod Is Dead

SERVES: 3–4

Juice of 2 medium limes

1 medium garlic clove, minced

1½ tsp ground cumin

¼ tsp garlic powder

¼ tsp ground cayenne pepper

1 tsp paprika

1 lb cod, cut into 2- or 3-inch pieces, depending on the size of your tortillas

Kosher salt to taste

Freshly ground black pepper to taste

1 tbsp coconut oil

12 to 15 4-inch corn tortillas, or 6 to 8 6-inch corn tortillas

¼ cup coarsely chopped cilantro (optional)

Chipotle Sauce

¼ cup mayonnaise

¼ cup sour cream

2 garlic cloves, minced

1 tbsp lime juice

2 tsp minced canned chipotle in adobo sauce, or more to taste

Pickled Shallots

2 shallots, halved and sliced thin

2 jalapeños, seeded, stemmed, and sliced into thin rings

1 cup white wine vinegar

2 tbsp lime juice

1 tbsp granulated sugar

1 tsp kosher salt

Lime Slaw

¼ head red cabbage, cored and sliced thin

¼ head green cabbage, cored and sliced thin

Juice of 1 lime

2 tbsp olive oil

¼ cup reserved liquid from Pickled Shallots

- In a glass bowl, combine lime juice, garlic, cumin, garlic powder, cayenne, and paprika. Mix well with a fork. Season cod on both sides with salt and pepper and place in the marinade. Toss until well coated and marinate for up to 30 minutes. While the fish is marinating you can prepare the sauce, pickled shallots, and slaw (see instructions on page 50).

- To cook fish, heat coconut oil in a skillet over medium heat. Add fish and sauté for about 3 minutes. Using a fish spatula or regular spatula, gently flip fish so that it doesn't flake and fall apart, and sauté for 3 minutes more. Transfer to a serving bowl.

- In a pan over medium-high heat, warm tortillas (2 to 3 at a time if small, or 1 if medium) on both sides. Stack tortillas on a plate and cover with a clean dishcloth to keep warm.
- To assemble tacos: place 1 piece of fish on a tortilla and top with lime slaw and pickled shallots. Drizzle with chipotle sauce and sprinkle with cilantro, if using.

For chipotle sauce:

- In a small bowl combine mayonnaise, sour cream, garlic, lime juice, and chipotle. Season with salt and pepper to taste. Refrigerate until ready to serve.

For pickled shallots:

- In a medium bowl combine shallots and jalapeños. In a small saucepan combine vinegar, lime juice, sugar, and salt and bring to a boil over medium-high heat until sugar has dissolved. Pour vinegar mixture over shallots and jalapeños and let sit for at least 30 minutes. Reserve ¼ cup of the pickling liquid for the slaw and discard the rest. Pickled shallots can be made and refrigerated up to 2 days in advance.

For lime slaw:

- Place cabbage in a large bowl. In a small bowl, whisk together lime juice, olive oil, and reserved pickling liquid. Pour lime mixture over cabbage, season with salt and pepper to taste, and toss to combine. Refrigerate until ready to serve.

Macaroni and Socracheese

Chidi: "So, making decisions isn't exactly my strong suit."
Michael: "I know that, buddy. You once had a panic attack at
a make-your-own sundae bar."

—Season 2, Episode 1, "Everything Is Great"

What constitutes the best macaroni and cheese dish? Oven-baked casserole or single pot on the stovetop? What's the ideal cheese? What's the ideal noodle shape? Why do some people insist on adding bread crumbs? For comfort-food aficionados, the great macaroni and cheese debate is right up there with the trolley problem; whole books and forums have been devoted to the subject. How can we possibly determine the best way to combine different combinations of cheeses with a seemingly endless variety of noodles?

It's the kind of decision that would make Chidi's stomach hurt. Time to employ the Socratic method.

A SOCRATIC DIALOGUE ABOUT NOODLES

Mac: The only good way to make macaroni and cheese is on the stove with elbow noodles.

Socrates: You clearly have opinions about this dish. Can you help me to understand the nature of your preferences?

Mac: Sure, I can explain why I'm right.

Socrates: What is the reason for elbow noodles?

Mac: The cheese sticks to the texture and fills the hole!

Socrates: Are there not other noodles with holes where cheese could collect?

Mac: Yes—

Socrates: Are there not other noodles with textures that would hold cheese?

Mac: Yes, but elbows are the ones I had as a kid.

Socrates: You make a lot of choices based on childhood preferences?

Mac: I mean, yeah. Flavors remind me of happier times.

Socrates: You clearly value nostalgia. What would be an example of a flavor that you did not like as a child, but like now?

Mac: Garlic. I hated stinky foods as a kid. But garlic makes everything better. I love it on everything now.

Socrates: So you would say that a dish with garlic would be better than one without garlic?

Mac: Pretty much.

Socrates: Would rigatoni and cheese with garlic be better than elbow noodles and cheese without garlic?

Mac: Oooh, I see what you did there.

In ancient Greece and Rome, philosophy was studied as a way to live a good life. Like Eleanor and her friends in the afterlife, early philosophers weren't just talking about ideas in the abstract; they were trying to put them into practice. Philosophy was a lifestyle choice, and the Socratic method of questioning was meant to inspire critical thinking and reflection as a way to challenge assumptions and improve oneself.

What we know of Socrates's life and teachings come to us from his student, Plato, who recorded them in his dialogues. In Plato's *Protagoras*, Hippocrates asks Socrates what nourishes the soul, to which Socrates replies, "Knowledge is the food of the soul." If that's true, then with each reboot and challenge they face together, Michael and the Good Place bunch are definitely getting fuller and fuller in their soul's bellies.

Just as there are many approaches to moral philosophy, there are many paths to cheesy pasta bliss. Eleanor might very well fall on the from-a-box side of the spectrum; Jason might opt for jalapeño-infused Velveeta; Tahani's palate might include a particular blend of fontina, gruyere, and gorgonzola with a sprinkle of panko. How can we choose? Asking open-ended, clear, and provocative questions can help us get to the heart of the matter. What tools and ingredients do we have at our disposal? What kind of eating experience are we looking for? Adventurous? Comforting? Quick and easy?

Our heavenly version combines the sweetness of caramelized onions with the richness of roasted garlic. We present . . .

Macaroni and Socracheese

V

SERVES: 6 (makes 42 Macaroni and Socracheese Bites)

1 head garlic

Olive oil to taste

Kosher salt to taste

Freshly ground black pepper to taste

8 oz elbow macaroni

1 cup bread crumbs, divided

½ cup (1 stick) unsalted butter, divided, plus
   extra to grease the pan

1 large onion, thinly sliced

¼ cup all-purpose flour

1½ cups whole milk

½ tsp mustard powder

⅛ tsp paprika, preferably Hungarian (sweet)

4 oz extra-sharp cheddar cheese, grated

4 oz havarti cheese, grated

¼ cup grated parmesan cheese

- Preheat oven to 400 degrees Fahrenheit. Line a sheet pan with foil. Peel the out-
  er layers and slice off, but do not discard, the top third of the head of garlic. Place
  garlic on the prepared pan. Drizzle with olive oil and season with salt and pepper.
  Replace the top of the garlic and wrap the foil tightly around it. Roast for 40
  minutes. Set aside and lower oven temperature to 350 degrees. Once the garlic is
  cool enough to handle, unwrap the foil, squeeze the cloves into a bowl, and use the
  back of a spoon to mash into a paste. (This step can be done a day in advance.)

- Bring a large pot of well-salted water to a boil. Boil the macaroni just shy of al
  dente, or several minutes less than the recommended cooking time. (The pasta
  will continue to cook in the oven.) Drain and rinse the macaroni under cold water
  to stop cooking. Place in a large bowl and set aside.

- Butter the wells of 2 mini muffin pans. Sprinkle about ½ cup of bread crumbs
  evenly among the muffin cups.

- In a large skillet over medium heat, melt 2 tablespoons of the butter. Add onions
  and sauté until browned, translucent, and tender, approximately 25 to 30 minutes. Don't rush this process. Stir every few minutes, allowing them to stick to the
  pan and brown but not burn. Reduce the heat to keep them from drying out, and
  feel free to add a little water to the pan, if needed. Set aside.

- In a medium saucepan over medium heat, melt the remaining 6 tablespoons
  of butter. Once bubbling, add flour and garlic paste. Whisk continuously for 4
  minutes to make a golden-brown roux. This will be the foundation of your Mornay
  sauce.

- Slowly add the milk, whisking until smooth. When the mixture seems blended but
  still thin, raise heat to medium-high and whisk often until bubbles form along the

edges and the mixture begins to thicken. Lower the temperature before it comes to a boil and simmer for approximately 5 minutes, until mixture is thick and gravy-like. Add the mustard powder and paprika. Season with salt and pepper to taste.

- Add small handfuls of cheeses a little at a time, stirring constantly to incorporate each addition. Continue to stir until cheese has melted thoroughly into the sauce. Remove from heat.

- Pour Mornay sauce over the cooked macaroni and gently toss until noodles are completely coated.

- Spoon a little macaroni and cheese mixture into each muffin cup, filling to the top. Sprinkle with the remaining ½ cup bread crumbs.

- Bake for 10 minutes. Remove from oven, top with caramelized onions, and bake for 5 more minutes.

- Remove pans from oven. Using a spatula gently remove mac and cheese bites from pan and transfer to a wire rack. Allow to cool for 5 minutes before serving.

NOTE: *To adapt the recipe for regular-sized muffin tins, cook for 10 minutes total after adding the onions. This makes approximately 14 large muffins.*

Schrödinger's Dog with Schopenhauerkraut

"I seem to be losing my ability to sustain object permanence. So it's sort of a glass half full, glass stops existing in time and space kind of deal."

—Janet, Season 2, Episode 6, "Janet and Michael"

When people hear the name Erwin Schrödinger, they usually think about his cat. Or, rather, the thought experiment known as Schrödinger's cat, in which we imagine that a cat is placed in a sealed box with poison and a radioactive substance. According to one interpretation of quantum mechanics, there's a point at which the cat could theoretically be alive *and* dead at the same time, yet when you open the box, it'll either be alive or dead. The thing to remember is: the cat was only hypothetically there in the first place.

Schrödinger's cat is a thought experiment about quantum physics and contradictions. The Nobel Prize–winning Austrian physicist created it in 1935 in response to the Copenhagen interpretation of quantum mechanics, which stated that an object in a system could exist in all possible configurations at the same time—it's only the observation of that object that collapses possibilities and forces the system into a single state. There's no way to observe that idea in the real world, though. Schrödinger designed his thought experiment to illustrate how absurd the train of thought could become. The point of Schrödinger's cat is, no one knows if any scientific theory is correct or wrong until it can be tested and proved.

In his 1944 book *What Is Life*, Schrödinger further discusses how the universe is given meaning through humans' attempts to understand it. Schrödinger's work and writing are rich in contradictions: realistic and idealistic, scientific and mystical, physical and quantum mechanical.

Schrödinger was also a devotee of the German philosopher Arthur Schopenhauer, who believed that the essence of all things is will, a wanting or longing that defines us. Influenced by Eastern thought, as well as by Plato and Kant, Schopenhauer developed philosophical pessimism: the idea that all life is longing and suffering, and all existence is a struggle to take from other organisms. The place where humanity can temporarily avoid pain is by making or appreciating art.

In Season 3, Episode 11, Eleanor and friends land in what appears to be a liminal space on the threshold of the Good Place, separated by a door that they're not allowed to pass through because, as the Good Place postal worker Gwendolyn tells them, "The only door for humans is the Official Entrance, which is a trillion miles north-south-north of here. So, you're kinda just stuck inside." In this way, the Good Place is a little like Schrödinger's cat, both there and not there. They won't know for sure until they open the door . . . which they're not allowed to do.

CORN DOG OR CORN PUPPY? SURPRISE!

Schrödinger: Please, try one of these corn dogs. Or, as the case might be, a corn puppy.

Schopenhauer: What's the difference?

Schrödinger: There is no difference. Each tubular corn fritter either contains a hot dog or doesn't—or both simultaneously. All statements are true at this moment, and the treats are indistinguishable from the outside.

Schopenhauer: But what if I want a hot dog?

Schrödinger: Then you might be disappointed.

Schopenhauer: I'm usually disappointed. You probably want all the hot dogs for yourself.

Schrödinger: Not so. I only speak the truth.

Schopenhauer: I hate surprises. That's why I bought sauerkraut. You know what you're getting with sauerkraut. It's right there in the name.

Schrödinger: I thought you believed in renouncing all desires? Salvation in resignation and all that?

Schopenhauer: That's the goal. There's also art, and cooking is a kind of art. It helps to ease the burden and boredom of life.

Schrödinger: I'm happy to share in easing your burden.

Schrödinger's Dog with Schopenhauerkraut

V GF

SERVES: 8–10

Corn Dogs

Vegetable oil for frying

8 hot dogs (beef franks or veggie), dried with
  paper towels and cut into fifths

1 cup corn flour (masa harina)

1 cup all-purpose or gluten-free flour

1 tbsp baking powder

¼ to ⅓ cup honey (use more if you like
  a sweet corn dog)

¼ tsp kosher salt

¼ tsp ground black pepper

1 large egg

1 to 1½ cups buttermilk, as needed

½ cup cornstarch

Schopenhauerkraut

4 tbsp salted butter or vegetable oil

1 medium onion, sliced into ½-inch rings

1 large carrot, grated

1 32-oz jar sauerkraut, drained

1 tsp mustard powder

1 cup golden raisins

Kosher salt to taste

Freshly ground black pepper to taste

- Preheat the oven to 200 degrees Fahrenheit. Line two large baking sheets with parchment paper. Set a cooling rack over one baking sheet on top of the parchment and place pan near your frying station. Place the other pan in the oven to warm.

- In a large pot heat about 3 inches of vegetable oil until the temperature reads 350 to 375 degrees Fahrenheit on a candy thermometer.

- In a large bowl, stir to combine flours, baking powder, honey, salt, and pepper. Stir in egg and 1 cup of the buttermilk. The batter should be a similar texture to pancake batter. If it seems too thick, add more buttermilk. Keep in mind that it will thicken as it stands so be prepared to add more as you work.

- Pour cornstarch into a shallow bowl. With your hands, gently roll each hot dog in cornstarch and shake off excess.

- Then dip into the batter and coat evenly. (Have napkins handy; this gets messy quickly.)

- In batches of 4 to 5, carefully drop battered hot dogs into the oil and fry for 2 to 3 minutes each, turning to ensure even cooking, until the batter is golden.

- Using a heatproof slotted spoon transfer the corn dogs to the prepared pan near the stove. Once the batch has been drained of excess oil, transfer to the pan in the oven. Keep warm while you cook the remaining hot dogs.
- After the corn dogs are cooked, make the corn puppies: Use an ice cream scoop to drop scoops of the leftover batter into the oil, again working in batches of 4 or 5. Fry for 4 to 5 minutes each until golden. Use a heatproof slotted spoon to transfer cooked corn puppies to the cooling rack. Once they're drained of excess oil, transfer to the pan in the oven.
- To make the Schopenhauerkraut, in a skillet over medium-low heat, melt butter. Add onions and sauté until translucent, approximately 15 minutes. Add carrots and cook for an additional 5 minutes. Stir in sauerkraut, ½ cup water, and mustard powder.
- Cover, reduce heat to medium-low, and cook for 15 minutes, stirring occasionally. Stir in raisins and another ½ cup water. Season with salt and pepper to taste. Cover and cook for another 45 minutes, stirring every 15 minutes.
- Transfer to a serving bowl and serve warm with corn dogs and corn puppies.

NOTE: *Schopenhauerkraut can be prepared ahead of time, refrigerated, and reheated on the stove.*

Karl's Poppers
with Ranch Tahani Sauce

Eleanor: "We're doing one small murder-y thing for a bigger, better reason. The ends justify the means."
Chidi: "Do you know who said that?"
Eleanor: "Was it someone nice and great, like Oprah?"

—Season 1, Episode 7, "The Eternal Shriek"

Sir Karl Raimund Popper had opinions about utopias. The science philosopher believed that so-called utopian engineering was fundamentally flawed. If some group or government was trying to achieve a perfect state, it might do so at the expense of anyone or anything that stood in its way. This approach is dangerously close to Machiavelli's idea that the ends justify the means, and Machiavelli is definitely in the Bad Place.

So perhaps the elaborate system of points that governs who gets into the Good Place is flawed utopian engineering?

Popper proposed an alternative to utopian engineering: the idea of "piecemeal social engineering." This approach to building a good world takes a narrower focus—much like creating a neighborhood. Popper believed social reform must start with one organization or institution at a time. The larger and broader the scope of that social reform—like, say, Michael's attempt to revamp the moral order of the universe—the greater the danger of things never getting done, such as in the Season 3 episode in which a Good Place committee is assembled to look into the point system. They discover that it would take 1,400 years just to recruit and vet a fully unbiased investigative team.

Michael, like Karl Popper, decides that small groups can enact change more quickly.

A POPPERATIC DIALOGUE ABOUT JALAPEÑOS

Hal: The best jalapeño poppers are from Buffalo Wild Wings in Jacksonville.

Karl Popper: Are they really the best? Maybe we could try to make a new kind of

---

popper, one that deconstructs the original and uses the best parts of it to make something new and different?

Hal: Why would we do that?

Karl: The search for truth is one of the strongest motives for scientific discovery. What are the best elements of a jalapeño popper?

Hal: The peppers need to be spicy, the cheese needs to be cheesy. Those are the most important things: spicy and cheesy.

Karl: What do you wish could be improved?

Hal: I wish they didn't get soggy and greasy so quickly. And there isn't a great way to save them if you don't eat them all at once. And my mom thinks they're too spicy.

Karl: What if there were a way to add them to something, like a small bite of chewy dough to hold the peppers and cheese, like a perfect little pocket?

Hal: A popper pocket?

Karl: Yes, a small container for the spicy, cheesy goodness.

Hal: That could work. What about the ranch?

Karl: You like tahini?

Hal: Who doesn't?

Karl: Try dipping your poppers in this ranch for a twist on the Buffalo experience.

Popper once wrote, "Those among us who are unwilling to expose their ideas to the hazard of refutation do not take part in the scientific game." He believed that theories and systems need to be constantly reviewed and evaluated.

Thankfully, the Judge who oversees decisions affecting the Good Place and the Bad Place seems to be reasonable and open to reviewing the system of who goes where. After observing and gathering information about the lives of human beings, she concludes, "Earth stinks, y'all," and agrees to help Michael reinvent his experiment.

Likewise, we have reviewed Jason's beloved jalapeño poppers, and we've combined their flavor with the crispy outside and chewy, delicious inside of Brazilian popovers. An improvement? We think so, but you'll have to repeat the experiment and evaluate it for yourself.

NOTES: *This recipe requires tapioca flour, which many grocery stores carry under the Bob's Red Mill brand. Before measuring the tahini to make the dipping sauce, be sure to stir the tahini well to incorporate any oil that has separated. This will help ensure a smooth dipping sauce.*

Karl's Poppers

SERVES: 6–8

¾ cup whole milk

¼ cup (½ stick) salted butter

1½ tsp kosher salt

2 cups tapioca flour

2 large eggs, room temperature

1 cup grated cheddar cheese

¼ cup canned sliced and pickled jalapeños (or more to taste), drained and quartered

Ranch Tahani

¼ cup tahini, well stirred

2 tbsp mayonnaise

2 tbsp lemon juice

3 tsp pure maple syrup

1 tsp stone-ground mustard, or ½ teaspoon mustard powder

1 tsp garlic powder

⅛ tsp celery salt

¼ tsp kosher salt, plus more to taste

⅛ tsp black pepper, plus more to taste

1 sprig fresh dill, finely chopped

- Preheat the oven to 400 degrees Fahrenheit. Grease the wells of a 12-cup muffin pan or mini muffin pan with butter or oil.
- In a large saucepan over medium heat, cook milk, butter, and salt until butter melts and mixture just begins to boil. Remove from heat.
- Transfer mixture to a large mixing bowl or a stand mixer fitted with the hook attachment. Gradually add flour to bowl, mixing vigorously with a wooden spoon or with the mixer on medium-low speed until incorporated. Let batter cool for 5 minutes. Then gently mix in eggs and cheese. Don't overmix. Batter will be runny but lumpy. Stir in jalapeños by hand.
- Fill each well of the prepared pan with batter. They should be full so that the poppers expand over the top of the pan while baking. Bake for 5 minutes, then lower oven temperature to 350 degrees and bake for 25 minutes.
- While poppers bake, make the ranch tahani: In a bowl whisk together tahini, mayonnaise, lemon juice, maple syrup, mustard, and 3 tablespoons water. Add garlic powder, celery salt, salt, and pepper. Taste and add salt and pepper as desired. Gently stir in dill. Serve or refrigerate until ready to use.
- Remove poppers from oven. Let cool for 10 minutes before serving.

NOTE: *If you would like to serve the tahini sauce as a dressing rather than a dip, add a few more teaspoons of water and whisk to desired consistency.*

I Think, Therefore I "Clam" Chowder

"It's just hot ocean milk with dead animal croutons."

—Eleanor, Season 2, Episode 2, "Dance Dance Resolution"

J anet is the cheerful, smiling manifestation of eternity's operating system. Over the time she spends with Eleanor and the rest of the Soul Squad, Janet's universal knowledge becomes slowly imbued with humanlike feelings. In Season 3, Janet attempts to save her friends from being abducted to the Bad Place by whisking their souls into her metaphysical void, which no other Janet has ever done before. When their souls reappear in Janet's void, Eleanor, Chidi, Tahani, and Jason all look like Janet. Why?

We turn to the philosopher and mathematician René Descartes for the answer. Descartes questioned everything—including his own existence. He argued that although we perceive our bodies through the use of our senses, these senses have been shown to be unreliable. Therefore, the only thing we can say with certainty is that we are thinking things, and that fact is how we know we exist. In other words, he said: "I think, therefore I am." We are embodied souls, he concluded; our souls and our bodies are not the same thing, though one resides inside the other.

THE GHOST IN THE NOT-A-MACHINE

In 1949, the philosopher Gilbert Ryle ridiculed Descartes's ideas about mind-body dualism, calling the proposition "the dogma of the ghost in the machine." Ryle argued that Descartes was mistaken in assuming that "mind" and "body" were the same category of thing. Rather, Ryle argued that they were not and, thus, that it makes no sense to analyze their relationship. As an alternative, he suggested that the body does not behave as a response to the mind manipulating the body; instead, the body's behavior *is* the functioning of the mind.

Regardless of who's right, the effects of fracturing the connection between the mind and body causes catastrophic effects on the humans in Janet's void, and the only way to restore wholeness is by forcing the mind to recognize the body.

What happens to our four humans when they lose their bodies (again) and find themselves in Janet-like bodies?

Eleanor's sense of self, and her basic consciousness, begins to break down once she loses her recognizable identity. Conversely, Janet is full of the thoughts and souls of the others, yet she begins to experience a breakdown of her own; her void literally starts to come apart at the seams.

There's a disconnect between who the humans are in their minds and what they see in their "bodies." Eleanor-Janet starts flipping through different bodies as she attempts to identify as . . . someone. Chidi tries to bring the true Eleanor back by reminding her of her memories, but ultimately it's something physical that ties her mind to the right body: a kiss.

As soon as they figure out how to reclaim their whole selves, Janet's void can no longer hold the dead humans because the void is only meant for Janet. Once they're expelled, Janet's wholeness is restored, and so is the Soul Squad's.

What does all this have to do with clam chowder?

The word *chowder* comes from the French word *chaudière*, which is related to the Old Northern French word *caudron*—or, in plain English, cauldron. The cauldron is known in mythology as a magical vessel, often a place where the dead can be revived.

Imagine that clam chowder is the breakdown of Janet's void. Things that don't actually belong together are smashing against each other in a white backdrop of perfect potential. The chowder could be good . . . in theory. But for that to happen, we need to remove the things that don't belong there, the misplaced bits that are throwing it all into chaotic collapse. We have to remove the clams.

Our vegan clam chowder restores balance in a rich and delicious broth by creating a perfect synthesis of nourishing plant-based ingredients. Without animal products, there are no "ghosts" and there is no dualism; there is only the transcendent experience of deliciousness.

I Think, Therefore I "Clam" Chowder   VG GF

SERVES: 8 large bowls, or 16 small bowls or cups

1 cup raw cashews

16 oz mushrooms (any kind), sliced

6 tbsp olive oil, divided

2 tsp Old Bay seasoning, divided

Kosher salt to taste

Freshly ground black pepper to taste

2 medium russet potatoes, peeled and cut into 1-inch pieces

1 tsp dried thyme

1 large yellow onion, sliced

2 garlic cloves, minced

3 tsp gluten-free tamari or gluten-free soy sauce, divided

2 cups unsweetened cashew milk (or any plant-based milk), divided

3 cups vegetable broth, divided, plus more as desired

2 celery stalks, diced

2 medium carrots, diced

⅓ tsp ground cayenne pepper

⅓ tsp paprika

1 cup dry white wine

3 tbsp all-purpose or gluten-free flour

2 tsp kelp granules or crumbled dulse flakes

2 tbsp freshly squeezed lemon juice (optional)

Bread or crackers for serving

Nutritional yeast or chopped parsley for garnish (optional)

- Place cashews in a bowl and cover with 2 inches of cold water. Soak overnight in the refrigerator. Drain cashews; they should be plump but hold their shape. Set aside.
- Preheat the oven to 425 degrees Fahrenheit. Line two baking sheets with parchment paper.
- In a bowl toss the mushrooms with 1 tablespoon of the olive oil, 1 teaspoon of the Old Bay, ½ teaspoon salt, and black pepper to taste. Spread onto one of the prepared pans in a single layer.
- In another bowl toss the potatoes with another 2 tablespoons of the olive oil, thyme, ½ teaspoon salt, and black pepper to taste. Spread onto the other prepared pan in a single layer.
- Bake the mushrooms for 20 minutes and the potatoes for 30 minutes, tossing both halfway through so they cook evenly. Set aside.
- In a Dutch oven or large stock pot over medium-low heat, heat another 2 tablespoons of the olive oil. Add onions and garlic and sauté for 10 minutes. Add 1 teaspoon of the tamari and sauté for 2 more minutes.

- Transfer onions and garlic to a large bowl and add potatoes, cashews, 1 cup of the cashew milk, and 1 cup of the vegetable broth. Using an immersion blender or food processor, blend mixture until smooth and thick. Set aside.
- In the same pot, heat the remaining 1 tablespoon of olive oil. Add celery, carrots, another 1 teaspoon of the tamari, cayenne, and paprika. Sauté until tender, 8 to 10 minutes. Add wine and the remaining teaspoon of Old Bay. Bring to a rapid boil, then lower to a simmer, and cook until the liquid is reduced by half, about 5 minutes.
- Add flour and stir constantly for 2 minutes, until vegetables are coated. Add 1 tablespoon of vegetable broth and stir constantly until creamy, about 5 minutes. Add the remaining vegetable broth, cashew milk, and tamari and the kelp granules. Stir well. Add the reserved potato mixture and stir until combined.
- Stir in mushrooms and cook over low heat for 10 to 15 minutes. Season with salt and pepper to taste. Add lemon juice if using. For a thinner chowder, add vegetable broth ½ cup at a time until you reach the desired consistency.
- Serve chowder with bread or crackers, and garnish with nutritional yeast flakes or parsley as desired.

NOTE: *Kelp granules and dulse flakes are forms of seaweed. You can find them at your local Asian mart or order them online at retailers likes Amazon. If you can't find them, substitute 1 teaspoon white miso.*

Francis Bacon's Rapt Dates

"Science is all about getting answers. You philosophers can spend your entire life mulling over a single question. That's why everyone hates moral philosophy professors."

—Simone, Season 3, Episode 1, "Everything Is Bonzer"

The Renaissance philosopher and founding father of modern science Sir Francis Bacon believed that our sensory experiences provide the best way to form an understanding of the world. As food lovers, we have to say: he had a point. Bacon developed a method for scientific inquiry using experiments to collect data that would, in turn, provide tangible proof to generalize and confirm an observed pattern. In his written work *Novum Organum*, Bacon details this system of inductive reasoning and argues that true knowledge is only attainable by its application.

In Season 2, Michael uses a form of inductive reasoning with the Judge, arguing that the many reboots in his neighborhood experiment represent a large data sample that proves, through repeated demonstration, that humans are able to improve their moral practices in the afterlife. Again and again, he has observed Chidi, Eleanor, Tahani, and Jason working together to become better people. Eight hundred reboots make a pretty strong inductive argument.

AN INDUCTION INTRODUCTION

Sir Francis Bacon [*sits*]: Hello. Are you my date?

Francis's Date: Hi! This is so exciting. I have to tell you, I'm a huge Bacon fan!

Bacon: Well, shucks. [*blushes*] Shall we order an appetizer? I bet you'll love the bacon flight.

Date: How can you be so sure?

Bacon: Inductive reasoning!

Date: What's that?

Bacon: It's the process of coming up with a universal conclusion by extrapolating

data made from an increasing number of instances. For example, I've met hundreds of human beings who like bacon. You're human, so I figure there's a good chance you like bacon.

Date: That . . . happens to be true, but it seems like kind of a weak argument.

Bacon: Ah, you're paying attention! You're right, that's the thing about inductive reasoning: it can lead to some pretty weak conclusions if the person doing the thinking is being lazy. But provide enough supporting evidence, and induction will take your hand and lead you straight to a conclusion as strong as the Rock of Gibraltar.

Date: Oh, you're so poetic. Like Shakespeare.

Bacon: Hardly. Question: How do you feel about dates?

Date: The sweet food like a giant raisin? Sure!

Bacon: OK, so you like bacon, and you like dates, so you'd probably like recipes made from bacon and dates. Would you say that's a weak argument or a strong one?

Date: My love for bacon is strong, and so is my love for dates. So I'll guess that this is a strong argument.

Bacon: The only way to know for sure is to test out a flight of bacon-date combinations and see what we can extrapolate.

Date: A flight?

Bacon: You've heard of a beer flight, right? A flight is another way of saying a collected sampling of things. We'll order a flight of bacon-wrapped dates because it will provide us with three different examples for collecting data. The more instances, the stronger the argument.

Date: Let's do it!

What is the best way to enjoy bacon-wrapped dates? We offer three examples for testing and evaluation. What will you be able to generalize after collecting your facts? You might need to repeat this experiment a few times, though fewer than eight hundred. We promise.

Francis Bacon's Rapt Dates

SERVES: 8

24 pitted Medjool dates

12 slices cooked uncured bacon, halved

2 oz manchego cheese, sliced into 16 pieces the size of almond slivers

8 fresh mint leaves

Sriracha to taste

Honey to taste

2 tbsp goat cheese

Tamari to taste

- Preheat oven to 350 degrees Fahrenheit. Line a baking sheet with aluminum foil.
- Divide the dates into three groups of 8. Each group will have a different filling.

For mint-filled dates:

- Press one mint leaf against the opening of each of the 8 dates (where the pits once were) and top with a slice of manchego. If your mint leaves are particularly large, tear the leaves so they're the same size as the dates. Slide both into the date and pinch the date to close it. Wrap each date with a piece of bacon and secure with a wooden toothpick. Place on baking sheet, roughly one inch apart.

For sriracha-honey dates:

- Lay 8 pieces of bacon flat on a plate. Brush with a thin layer of sriracha. Place a slice of manchego into each of the 8 dates. Wrap each date in a piece of sriracha bacon with the sriracha side against the date. Secure with a toothpick. Drizzle each date with honey. Place on baking sheet, roughly one inch apart.

For tamari and goat cheese dates:

- Lay 8 pieces of bacon flat on a plate. Brush with a thin layer of tamari. Fill each date with a chickpea-sized amount of goat cheese. Roll each date in a piece of tamari bacon, with the tamari side against the date. Secure with a toothpick. Place on baking sheet, roughly one inch apart.
- Bake all dates uncovered for 3 to 4 minutes, then flip using tongs, and cook for another 3 minutes, or less if you prefer chewier bacon.
- Use tongs to transfer dates to serving plates. For a bacon flight, place one of each variety on 8 small plates. Let cool slightly before serving; remove toothpicks if you'd like.

Demon's Prawn

"Unless I can figure out a compelling reason to keep you here, you will spend eternity with murderers, and arsonists, and people who take off their shoes and socks on commercial airlines."

—Michael, Season 1, Episode 8, "Most Improved Player"

You would probably expect demons to at least make an appearance in a show about the afterlife, and you would be correct. Demons are the creative torturers of humans in the Bad Place; we've heard about a colorful array of their classic and favorite tortures, including:

- Penis flatteners
- Butthole spiders
- Pulling out your fingernails
- Throwing you into an acid pit
- Burying you up to the neck in a volcano of scorpions
- Removing brains, studying them, and batting them around a stadium like beach balls
- Making philosophers attend class naked during the day and hitting them with hammers all night
- Peeling arms like bananas
- Turning you inside out by reaching down your throat and grabbing your butt from the inside
- Serving only Hawaiian pizza
- An endless baby shower for a woman you don't know
- Locking you in a room for eternity with nothing to read but *New Yorker* magazines, and they'll just keep coming

In his 1641 treatise *Meditations on First Philosophy*, French mathematician and philosopher René Descartes presented the concept of Cartesian skepticism, which consists of doubting anything that cannot be proven through logic. He uses three arguments to make his point: the dream argument, the deceiving God argument, and the malicious demon argument. In the example of dreaming, he talks about how our senses perceive things to be real that are, in fact, false. The deceiving God argument refers to an all-powerful creator who, having the power to change reality, can therefore trick humans; however, Descartes rejects this idea on the principle that God is ultimately good and would not seek to deceive us. Descartes concludes with the malicious demon argument, which states that reality is being manipulated by a malevolent spectator that *isn't* God. In the case of *The Good Place*, it seems that the Soul Squad's destiny might well be controlled by such a Cartesian demon.

THE PLACE OF ALL DEMONS

The final episode of Season 3 gets its title, "Pandemonium," from John Milton's magnum opus, *Paradise Lost*, an epic poem about Lucifer, the first angel turned demon who defies his creator (God) and wages war on Heaven. Milton coined the word Pandæmonium, which translates into "the place of all demons," to refer to the palace built in the middle of Hell.

We have not yet heard about a palace in the Bad Place, but there are more than a few departments:

- Spastic Dentistry
- Disembowelment
- Children's Dance Recitals
- Holiday Weekend at Ikea
- Partial Decapitations
- Toxic Masculinity
- 9 Hot Dog Torture Departments (making people into, stuffing people with, etc.)

To celebrate Shawn, Vicky, Trevor, Chet, Bambadjan, and all the other demons, we bring you a little Demon's Prawn to spice things up. These shrimp have quite a lot of kick, but if you'd like to make this dish even spicier, increase the cayenne pepper to 1 teaspoon and the sriracha to 3 tablespoons—or more, if you're making it for residents of the Bad Place.

Demon's Prawn

SERVES: 4

2 tbsp salted butter

4 tbsp olive oil

4 garlic cloves, minced

1 tbsp curry powder, preferably vindaloo

½ tsp ground cayenne pepper, or to taste

1 tsp ground turmeric

2 tbsp dark brown sugar, packed

¼ tsp kosher salt, plus more to taste

1 tsp lime zest

2 tbsp lime juice

1 tsp smoked paprika

1 tbsp Worcestershire sauce

1 tsp liquid smoke

2 tbsp sriracha, or to taste

½ fresh pineapple, cut into 1-inch chunks, or 1 20-oz can pineapple chunks, drained

1 medium green bell pepper, cored, seeded, and cut into 1-inch pieces

1 lb raw shrimp, peeled and deveined (recommended: Key West pink shrimp)

1 tbsp chopped fresh parsley (optional)

Crusty french bread for serving

- In a large skillet over medium-low heat, heat butter and olive oil until butter melts and bubbles. Add garlic, curry powder, cayenne, and turmeric. Sauté for 2 to 3 minutes, until garlic and spices become fragrant.

- Reduce heat to medium. Add brown sugar, salt, lime zest and juice, paprika, Worcestershire, liquid smoke, and sriracha. Bring to a boil and simmer for 10 minutes, stirring occasionally.

- Add pineapple and peppers and sauté for 5 minutes. Add shrimp and cook until they are no longer translucent, 4 to 5 minutes.

- Use a slotted spoon to transfer shrimp, pineapple, and peppers to a serving bowl. Continue cooking the sauce for 4 to 5 minutes until it thickens. Then let cool for a minute and pour over the shrimp, pineapple, and peppers.

- Top with parsley, if using, and serve warm as a communal appetizer with slices of crusty french bread.

Kierkegaarden Salad on a Stick

"I know it sounds crazy. But if it weren't crazy, they wouldn't call it a leap of faith. They would call it a sit of doubting."

—Eleanor, Season 2, Episode 8, "Leap to Faith"

In Season 2, Episode 8, Michael's supernatural colleagues throw a party to celebrate the success of his neighborhood experiment. One of the events is a roast in which Michael says something profoundly mean about each of the humans. Despite his apparent betrayal, Eleanor insists that Michael hasn't abandoned them and they should not give up on him. The evidence that he's still on their side is thin, but it's enough to convince the humans to take what Kierkegaard called a "leap into faith" and risk trusting Michael again.

In his 1843 book *Fear and Trembling*, Søren Kierkegaard (writing pseudonymously as Johannes de Silentio) highlights the inadequacies of ethics. Kierkegaard used the biblical example of Abraham and Isaac to write about instances in which a person's faith in a particular, highly valued relationship demands that the individual suspend their usual ethical practices. He dubbed this paradox of faith the teleological suspension of the ethical.

Considered by many to be the first existential philosopher, Kierkegaard published most of his books under pen names. He used different monikers to explore variations in philosophical systems and, in doing so, left many holes for readers to discover, grow frustrated with, and ponder independently. The act of writing those different perspectives helped illustrate to the readers his point: it's up to the individual to figure out and live an authentic life of meaning.

PHILOSOPHY ON A STICK

In Seasons 1 and 2 of *The Good Place*, Michael's neighborhood features a lot of restaurants, with each reboot offering a different trend, including frozen yogurt, chowder, and a variety of "on a stick" restaurants: steak on a stick, bagel on a stick (see page 21 for our version), caviar on a stick, hot dog on a stick on a stick. But we don't see

Salad on a Stick . . .

Sal: I need to serve a salad to my father.

Johannes: You seem to have tasty ingredients there on the counter: lettuce, beets, celery, Danablu. Very nice—I approve. But what are you going to do with those bamboo skewers?

Sal: That's how I'm serving the salad.

Johannes: But . . . salads belong in bowls. There's no reason for them to be placed on a stick!

Sal: That's what Dad wants, and I want to make him happy.

Johannes: But that's not how salads are served.

Sal: I know, but he's my father and pleasing him is more important than social convention.

Johannes: That's a curious ethical justification for a salad delivery system.

Sal: Maybe so, but it's delicious.

Johannes: I suppose it *is* up to the individual, and truth lies in the search for an object, not in the object itself. So the making of this salad on a stick to please your father is what matters.

Sal: It's my leaf of faith.

Food on sticks isn't unusual, even if salad on a stick is. Cooking food on sticks connects humanity with our prehistoric ancestors, whose earliest attempts at cooking likely involved impaling bits of meat, fruits, and vegetables on a branch and heating them over a fire. As humans evolved, we developed other ways of preparing food, but the simplicity of skewered food never went away. From kebabs to canapes to lollipops to elote, there are plenty of examples of sweet and savory treats on a stick around the world.

One could say that food on sticks is a universal culinary absolute. Here we challenge the idea that a salad must be served in a bowl and reimagine it deconstructed and presented in a new way. With a Danish blue cheese chosen to honor the great Danish philosopher, this salad is simple but exceptional.

NOTE: *For this recipe you will need 24 bamboo skewers. Four- or six-inch skewers work well, but toothpicks are too short to hold all the salad ingredients.*

Kierkegaarden Salad on a Stick

GF

MAKES: 24 salads on a stick

½ head iceberg lettuce, cut into 24 small wedges

4 oz blue cheese (preferably a nice Danish one, like Danablu)

1 8-oz package cooked beets or 1 cup cooked and peeled beets, sliced thin

24 green seedless grapes

4 to 5 medium celery stalks, cut into 24 ½-inch pieces

6 slices bacon cooked but not too crispy, cut into 4-inch pieces (optional)

Mustard Vinaigrette

4 tbsp olive oil

2 tbsp white wine vinegar

1 tbsp stone-ground mustard

Kosher salt to taste

Freshly ground black pepper to taste

- Thread one wedge of lettuce onto a skewer. Top with approximately ½ teaspoon of blue cheese. Then add a piece of beet, one grape, a piece of celery, and a piece of bacon, if using. Arrange skewers on a serving platter.

- In a measuring cup or bowl, combine vinaigrette ingredients and whisk to incorporate. Gently drizzle dressing over the skewers.

Chives of Quiet Marination

"One man's waste is another man's water—and both men are me."

—Doug Forcett, Season 3, Episode 8, "Don't Let the Good Life Pass You By"

In 1845, then twenty-seven-year-old Henry David Thoreau went into the woods of Massachusetts to remove himself from the vigorous world of manufacture and commerce where, in his words, "the mass of men lead lives of quiet desperation." He wanted to live simply and alone in nature. This period of relative isolation in his cabin on Walden Pond inspired his 1854 book *Walden*, as well as his 1866 essay "Civil Disobedience," one of the most influential works in American history.

Does Thoreau's seclusion remind you of someone on *The Good Place*? Maybe the legendary Doug Forcett, the only human being ever to come close to guessing the points system of the afterlife? After a psychedelic-mushroom-inspired revelation, Doug also chooses to go "off the grid" to "live a perfect life," as Michael says.

Both men search for their version of utopia: one in the wilderness of Walden Pond, the other in the wilds of Calgary. Each one also serves as a blueprint and inspiration to others. Thoreau's ideas about a simpler life inspired writers, thinkers, and environmentalists who came after him. His nonanthropocentric ethic—the idea that all natural life has intrinsic value, including trees, plants, and animals—is echoed in Doug Forcett's empathy toward Martin Luther Gandhi Tyler Moore the snail and the other creatures memorialized in his animal graveyard.

Doug Forcett's personal philosophy elevated him to an unprecedented level of notoriety in the afterlife. Even Bad Place residents were in awe of the accuracy of Doug's theory of the moral point score. For Michael, Janet, and the Soul Squad, Doug becomes an exemplar of living thoughtfully and carefully. Doug tries to conform to a rigid, self-imposed system to maximize his afterlife points by making considerate choices and avoiding all behavior that could have negative repercussions. Whether or not this will get Doug into the Good Place is another matter.

It stands to reason that chives, with their delicate blades and fragrant aroma, carefully minced and placed into a small bowl of vinegar to gently marinate, can provide an opportunity to meditate on the small things.

Chives of Quiet Marination

SERVES: 6–8

4 tbsp minced chives, divided

4 tsp white wine vinegar

4 tbsp salted butter

1½ large onions, diced

1 tsp kosher salt, plus more to taste

1 tsp granulated sugar

2 cups sour cream

1 tsp lemon juice

Freshly ground black pepper to taste

Sliced vegetables or potato chips for serving

- Set aside ½ teaspoon of the chives. In a small bowl, combine the remaining chives with the vinegar. Marinate for 30 minutes.
- As the chives are (quietly) marinating, in a pan over medium heat melt the butter. Add the onions. Cover and cook, stirring occasionally, until they're translucent, 20 to 25 minutes.
- Add salt and sugar. Sauté for 15 more minutes uncovered, stirring occasionally. Add the chive-and-vinegar mixture to the pan and remove from heat. Let cool for 5 to 10 minutes.
- Transfer mixture to a medium bowl and stir in sour cream, lemon juice, and salt and pepper to taste. Top with the reserved chives.
- Cover and refrigerate dip for 30 minutes or until ready to serve.
- Serve with sliced veggies or potato chips for dipping. Ponder the fragile nature of existence and the beauty of nature.

Steak Stortles

"There have to be stakes, or it's just another thought experiment."

—Chidi, Season 2, Episode 5, "The Trolley Problem"

The stakes are high for the Soul Squad as they navigate the fake Good Place, the Bad Place, the Medium Place, and a few interdimensional spaces in between on their quest to get into the real Good Place. Their battle for a better afterlife isn't just about them; it's about all of humanity. The consequences are important.

In a steak recipe, the consequences are also important. Overcook the meat and the dish is tough, hard to chew, and bland. Undercook the steak, and you risk getting E. coli or another foodborne illness.

As Season 2, Episode 5 demonstrated, there is a difference between a thought experiment and its real-life application. In 1967 in the *Oxford Review*, the British philosopher Philippa Foot offered the trolley problem as a thought experiment to gauge the intuitive morality of killing one person to save five others. It requires making an impossible decision. Whom do you choose to save, and what gives you the right to do so?

In the second season of *The Good Place*, Chidi tries to teach Michael and the humans how to be better people. They discuss the trolley scenario, and everyone has an opinion about how it should play out. Trolley-related studies and experiments have been considered and adapted by philosophers around the world for nearly a half century, but Michael takes the trolleyology out of the realm of theoretical fatalities and forces Chidi to make real, on-the-spot decisions.

In the context of the trolley problem, as soon you make a choice you are complicit. Michael puts Chidi at the helm of their experiment and asks him to decide whom to save—and whom to sacrifice. Although the experiment is a construct, the Soul Squad's pain is real, and so is Chidi's anxiety.

CONSEQUENTIALISM VS. DEONTOLOGY VS. VIRTUE ETHICS

The term *consequentialism* is said to have been coined by Philippa Foot's friend and colleague Elizabeth Anscombe. In basic philosophical terms, consequentialism (a form of utilitarianism) is the idea that morality is based upon the goal of creating the best consequences. The means are not really important, as long as they produce a beneficial result.

Deontology argues that there are strict rules that people must follow in a functional society. The philosophy adopted and argued for by Foot, Anscombe, and their circle, however, was *virtue ethics*. With its roots in the works of Aristotle and Thomas Aquinas, this theory emphasized virtue of character and action.

While attempting to teach Eleanor and Jason, Chidi explains consequentialism as acting so as to cause the "most good and pleasure and the least pain and suffering."

In Season 3, we see examples of all three theoretical perspectives when the friends are back on Earth trying to cope with the idea that they're doomed to spend eternity in the Bad Place. Tahani and Jason give random Australians large sums of money in a good example of consequentialism; Eleanor returns a lost wallet in an act that exemplifies deontology. The conclusion that Eleanor comes to and offers to Chidi can ultimately be called an example of virtue ethics: the Soul Squad chooses to help other people not because it'll benefit them, but because it's the right thing to do.

In order for the steak in this recipe to get to a good place, deontology serves you best; here, it's important to follow the rules. As we learn from Season 3, meddling with the rules too much can have serious consequences. As the Judge tells the Soul Squad, "Do you know how much weird stuff has happened because of your little experiment? England left Europe. That Hugh Jackman musical about P. T. Barnum? It made like $400 million. Also, the Jacksonville Jaguars are good now. . . . I'm serious! They're going to make the playoffs. Blake Bortles is kind of okay, maybe—I don't know, it's being debated among experts, it's confusing. But whatever it is, it's your fault!"

These delicious crostini-like bite-sized sandwiches can also be your fault, with far more delicious consequences.

Steak Stortles

SERVES: 10–12

1½ lb flank steak, about 1 to 1½ inches thick, trimmed of excess fat

3 tbsp olive oil, divided

Kosher salt to taste

Freshly ground black pepper to taste

1 french baguette, cut into ¼-inch-thick slices (about 24 total)

2 tbsp store-bought creamy horseradish

⅔ cup sour cream

¼ cup stone-ground mustard

4 oz parmesan cheese, shaved into thin slices

8 oz roasted red peppers, drained and diced

- Preheat the oven to 350 degrees. Place the flank steak on a roasting pan or baking dish. Coat on all sides with 1 tablespoon of the olive oil and season well with salt and pepper. Let stand at room temperature.
- Arrange the baguette slices on a baking sheet and brush on both sides with olive oil. Season with salt and pepper. Toast until crisp and golden, approximately 10 minutes. Meanwhile, in a small bowl combine horseradish, sour cream, and mustard. Mix well and refrigerate until ready to serve.
- Transfer toasts to a platter and turn the oven temperature up to broil. Place the steak in the oven and cook for 4 to 5 minutes per side, depending on the thickness of the beef. The steak should be firm but pink in the center. Remove from oven and let rest for 5 minutes on the pan.
- Using a sharp knife cut the steak across the grain into thin, 2-inch-long slices.
- To assemble the crostini: Top each toast with 2 to 3 parmesan shavings, 1 to 2 slices of steak, a dollop of horseradish cream, and a few red peppers. Serve at room temperature.

Moral
Desserts

Candide Apples

"It turns out the best Janet was the Janet that was inside Janet all along."

—Janet, Season 1, Episode 3, "Tahani Al-Jamil"

As the German philosopher and mathematician Gottfried Leibniz saw it, the philosophy of optimism presents the possibility that the world we know is "the best of all possible worlds"—primarily because it is the only one we have. But this idea of making the best of things works only if one has the power and ability to make things better.

Optimists often believe that either things are already good enough or that they possess the ability to make them better. Optimists are helpers. The famous philosopher of neighborly love, Mister Rogers, once talked about how in times of crisis, there were always people trying to help. "Look for the helpers," he said, quoting his mother's advice.

The Good Place's Janet is a helper. In fact, she's *the* quintessential helper, and one might go so far as to call her the archetypal optimist; she seems to perceive every person, thing, and event as a unique and inherently meaningful part of the fabric of existence. Even though she's more knowledgeable and less judgmental than everyone around her, she moves through life (or, more accurately, the afterlife) without ego or vanity, and almost everything makes her smile. In Season 1, she tells Chidi that, as a Good Place Janet, she is "an anthropomorphized vessel of knowledge built to make your life easier."

Unlike Leibniz, Janet, and Mister Rogers, the philosopher Voltaire (born François-Marie Arouet) disagreed with the premise of optimism, so much so that in 1759 he wrote a famous parody of the concept, *Candide*, to refute the idea that human suffering is part of a benevolent cosmic plan. Voltaire mistrusted institutions, including churches. He believed in the idea of God but thought it likely that God created the world and then left it to us to do with as we will.

Sounds a little like Voltaire had a hand in writing *The Good Place*, where we've seen little evidence of a higher power, just inefficient bureaucracies. Voltaire believed that optimism and faith only go so far—at some point, you have to work on making things better yourself. The famous last line of his novel is, "That is very well put ... but we must cultivate our garden."

Which, naturally, brings us to apples.

Apples have played a significant role in stories about morality since Biblical times. Ancient Greek mythology tells us that Eris, the goddess of not getting along with people, once started a decade's worth of trouble by offering a prized apple to whoever was deemed the most beautiful goddess, which caused three goddesses with pride issues to escalate their pettiness into a full-blown Trojan War. And in the Book of Genesis, of course, the apple* in the Garden of Eden symbolizes humans' sacrifice of ignorant, obedient bliss in exchange for the knowledge and free will to make their own decisions and suffer the consequences.

*Not an apple.

Voltaire's *Candide* ends in the garden, which is both an allusion to the Garden of Eden and a place where humanity must work to make things grow and thrive. Left alone, a garden will not yield a bountiful harvest. Even the Good Place needs a Janet to help the community thrive, just like the Bad Place needs its own Janet, too. Our world, with its many challenges, injustices, and disasters, could use a few Janets to make it better.

Whether you believe in the optimism of Leibniz or the skepticism of Voltaire, one thing is for certain: life needs helpers. An apple may grow on a tree by the power of nature, but if you want enough apples to feed your family, and if you want to help the tree survive a drought, and if you want to use the apples to make tasty baked treats, you need to get involved. You need to be a helper. Like Janet.

Halfway between a compote and the traditional Jewish dish called charoset, Candide Apples is a treat that makes for an equally delightful dessert (served on cookies) or occasional breakfast (eaten with a spoon). Best of all, it respects *The Good Place* creator Michael Schur's passionate opinion that hot fruit, such as apple pie, is terrible. Candide Apples might share some flavors with apple pie, but they're made cold and served cold.

Candide Apples

V GF

SERVES: 4

2 Granny Smith apples, cored

½ tbsp lemon juice

1 15-oz can plums in syrup, drained and pitted

8 Medjool dates, pitted

1 cup pecans, crushed

⅓ cup honey

½ tbsp ground cinnamon

1 tsp ground ginger

Gingersnaps or gluten-free graham crackers for serving

- Cut the apples into ¼-inch cubes. In a medium bowl toss with the lemon juice.
- Cut plums and dates into ¼-inch cubes. Add to the bowl along with pecans.
- Stir in honey, cinnamon, and ginger until fruit is evenly coated.
- Spoon a heaping tablespoon of the apple mixture onto each cookie. Arrange cookies on a platter and serve as dessert bites.

Moral Dilemma Meringue Cookies

"There are so many unintended consequences to well-intentioned actions. It feels like a game you can't win!"

—Tahani, Season 3, Episode 10, "The Book of Dougs"

Are there times when the best of intentions result in harm? If so, does the good outweigh the bad? Philosopher and theologian Thomas Aquinas argued yes; one can justify an action that causes harm if the motivation is to accomplish a moral good. Aquinas first introduced this idea, called the doctrine of double effect, to justify using violence in self-defense, and it has since been used to explore the morality of everything from the death penalty to euthanasia.

In Season 2, Chidi experiences a teachable moment when discussing possible ways to deal with the Tahani-Jason-Janet love triangle. After Janet creates Derek, her rebound guy whose man-functioning existence threatens the humans' safety, Michael suggests killing Derek for the greater good. Chidi rejects that plan but applies the doctrine of double effect to justify breaking up Jason and Tahani's happy relationship in order to make Derek's existence unnecessary. Chidi decides that the couple's heartache is better than the suffering that all four humans would endure if they were discovered by the demons and sent to the Bad Place, so Eleanor tells the couple about Janet and Jason's marriage in Season 1 and Derek's creation. Derek is boxed up, and Janet begins to sort out her feelings.

MERINGUES

Crisp on the outside, a little chewy on the inside, these beautifully formed cookies are like magic. Whip egg whites with sugar and they're transformed into peaks that can be baked into beautiful, edible sculptures.

But there's a dark side to these innocent-looking treats. The doctrine of double effect is at play. To make meringues, you have to sacrifice the yolks for the good of the cookie. In fact, if any of the yolk gets into the white, the meringue won't form properly. Fortunately, you don't need to throw them away—you can set them aside for another recipe, like lemon curd, custard, hollandaise sauce, or crème brûlée. (Don't despair if you don't have a reason to use those yolks right now. For sweet recipes, mix four yolks with 1 teaspoon sugar water and freeze until ready to use. For savory dishes, combine 4 yolks with ⅛ teaspoon fine salt and freeze until ready to use.)

Moral Dilemma Meringue Cookies

V GF

MAKES: 24 large or 48 small cookies

4 large eggs

2 tsp cornstarch

¾ cup granulated sugar

1 tsp finely grated lemon zest

¼ tsp kosher salt

¼ tsp cream of tartar

1 tsp lemon extract

- Arrange two oven racks in the upper middle and lower middle positions in the oven. Preheat oven to 225 degrees Fahrenheit. Line two baking sheets with parchment paper.

- Set a small strainer over a small bowl. One at a time, carefully crack eggs into the strainer, letting the whites slide through into the bowl without any yolk (or the meringue won't set properly). Reserve yolks for another use. Allow egg whites to come to room temperature for 10 to 15 minutes.

- In a small bowl combine cornstarch with sugar and lemon zest. Set aside.

- Using a stand mixer fitted with the whisk attachment or a hand mixer, beat egg whites, salt, and cream of tartar on high speed until foamy. Carefully add dry ingredients and beat on high speed until mixture forms stiff, glossy peaks, 3 to 4 minutes, scraping down the sides of the bowl with a spatula as you go. Use a spatula to gently fold in the lemon extract.

- Transfer the meringue mix to a piping bag fitted with a large star tip or a gallon-sized plastic bag with one bottom corner carefully cut off. Pipe the meringue onto the prepared sheets in small swirls, about 1¼ inches in diameter.

- Bake for 30 minutes. Swap the tray from the top rack to the bottom, and vice versa; this will help cookies bake evenly. Bake for another 30 minutes. Turn off the oven and do not open the oven door. Let cookies cool in the oven for an hour.

- Store cookies in an airtight container for up to 2 weeks.

Chosen Yogurt Chocolate Camousse

Eleanor: "What is it with you and frozen yogurt?
Have you not heard of ice cream?"
Michael: "Oh, sure, but I've come to really like frozen yogurt.
There's something so human about taking something great
and ruining it a little so you can have more of it."

—Season 1, Episode 6, "What We Owe to Each Other"

C hidi is known to say "what?" whenever something crazy happens, which is a lot. Usually it's less a request for information than an exclamation in the face of epic befuddlement to assert his continued existence as a person who would like to have some sort of relationship with a comprehensible reality.

(Hey, when a dance-club DJ who once suffocated himself during a poorly thought-out robbery tells you he's getting married to the sentient manifestation of all knowledge in the universe, what are you *supposed* to say?)

The twentieth-century French philosopher Albert Camus called what we experience in this kind of moment *absurdism*: the conflict between our desperate need to find meaning in life and the fact that, apparently, the universe has none to offer us.

It does, however, offer us yogurt. So there's that.

THAT'S ABSURD

Absurdism is a philosophical perspective that seems well matched to fantastical sci-fi stories. Chidi's literary predecessors in cosmic bafflement include Arthur Dent from Douglas Adams's *The Hitchhiker's Guide to the Galaxy*, who survived Earth's destruction in his bathrobe only to have the commander of an alien space-demolition fleet read bad poetry to him. Billy Pilgrim from Kurt Vonnegut's *Slaughterhouse-Five* found himself experiencing his life out of chronological order and then was abducted by aliens to mate with a movie star in an extraterrestrial zoo. Alice from *Alice's Adventures in Wonderland* fell down a rabbit hole into a surreal realm where a pack of playing cards threatened her with decapitation. Good times!

When the humans arrive in the Good Place, they're bemused by the ubiquity of frozen yogurt. Shops with names like Yogurt Acres, Yogurt Horizons, and Yogurt Yoghurt Yogurté quickly reveal the afterlife's apparent fetish for bacterially fermented milk, which seems bizarre; here on Earth, fro yo is generally seen as a *less* heavenly substitute for ice cream.

But Eleanor and the others go with it. They're in the forking Good Place, after all—there must be a good reason why yogurt is the number one dessert of the afterlife. Of course, it turns out that Michael's trolling them. The humans read divine meaning into all that dairy but, in the end, it's totally meaningless.

The Soul Squad could've fallen into utter hopelessness after discovering they had been tricked by Bad Place demons. Fortunately, absurdism is different from nihilism (which Chidi briefly slips into later, in Season 3, with his big pot of *oh-well-fork-everything* chili; see page 47). Nihilism suggests that the meaninglessness of existence renders morality irrelevant—that no action is inherently more right or wrong than any other. Absurdism, on the other hand, offers a ray of light. Camus contended that although the universe gives no inherent meaning to life, the beauty we encounter in the world can make life worthwhile anyway—and personal integrity can function in place of universal morality.

We won't argue here that yogurt is inherently meaningful. We *will* point out that you can choose yogurt in place of eggs to make a simpler yet thoroughly lovely chocolate mousse. If that makes you say, "what?"—well, fine. Camus would probably suggest you roll with it.

Chosen Yogurt Chocolate Camousse

SERVES: 8

1 cup Greek yogurt

6 oz dark chocolate (about 50 percent cocoa content), chopped

½ cup whole milk

3 tbsp Kahlúa or other coffee-flavored liqueur

3 tbsp chopped hazelnuts

1 tbsp granulated sugar

½ cup heavy cream

- In a small heatproof bowl whisk yogurt until smooth.
- Place chocolate in a medium heatproof bowl. In a small saucepan over medium heat bring milk to a boil. Pour over chocolate and let stand for 2 minutes. Using a small plastic spatula stir gently until smooth. Fold in yogurt. Stir in liqueur.
- Spoon into eight small custard cups or large shot glasses and freeze for 1 hour.
- While mousse is chilling, make the hazelnut whipped cream: In a small bowl, combine nuts, sugar, and heavy cream. Use a hand mixer to whip until smooth. Refrigerate until ready to use.
- Top each mousse cup with a large dollop of whipped cream.

Somebody Important's Angel Pie

**"You know, I haven't been this upset since my good friend
Taylor was rudely upstaged by my other friend, Kanye,
who was defending my best friend, Beyoncé."**

—Tahani, Season 1, Episode 8, "Most Improved Player"

S cholars do it. Socialites do it. Philosophers do it. Everyone name-drops. People tag famous "friends" on Facebook and Instagram. They slip the name of influential friends into conversations. But why?

Name-dropping—the seemingly natural mention of a famous person's name—is a way for people to call attention to a relationship for the purpose of elevating their own status or credibility.

Tahani Al-Jamil is a perpetual name-dropper, wielding famous associations to call attention to her high social standing and value. Princess Diana was her godmother; she was Baz Luhrmann's muse; she snogged Ryan Gosling twice; James Cameron gave her the Heart of the Ocean necklace; she set up her good friend Drake with her other good friend Ruth Bader Ginsburg; Malala Yousafzai and Kylie Minogue wrote the foreword to her published diary; and the Dalai Lama sent her inspirational texts.

Name-dropping is a way of placing oneself within a hierarchy, often to emphasize superiority but also credibility. In many ways, *The Good Place*'s writers do the same thing as Tahani; all those allusions to philosophers in the show—on the blackboard, in conversations, and on strategically placed books—are a form of name-dropping that give the show a layer of thoughtful, philosophical legitimacy. Such references demonstrate to the audience that the writers have done their homework and that they're positioning the show in a continuum of philosophical discussion that comments on life and death, ethics and entertainment.

The philosophers name-dropped on *The Good Place* (and in this cookbook)—many dead, some alive—are considered authorities, thus lending the Soul Squad's story gravitas it wouldn't have otherwise. This is what Tahani yearns for whenever she mentions famous friends like Princess Grace, Vanessa Redgrave, and Johnny Depp.

The beauty of this confection is that you can tailor it to satisfy all your name-dropping needs by changing both the filling and the name to fit your particular situation. Might Janelle Monáe have brought you a basket of peaches from Georgia? Then make Janelle's Peach Angel Pie. Got some delicious honey from Neil Gaiman's beehive? Make Neil's Honey Angel Pie. Some fresh squash from Billy Corgan? That naturally requires making Smashing Pumpkins' Angel Pie. Mike Schur brings you a bunch of freshly roasted coffee beans? Schur's Mocha Angel Pie. The options are endless.

Our decadently sweet version comes from the kitchens of one of New Jersey's well-established historical families. Thanks, Stu Segal of the Atlantic City Youtie-Segals, for sharing your recipe for Stu's Boardwalk Butterscotch Angel Pie.

NOTES: *Use a "deep dish" 9½-inch pie pan, which is 1½ inches deep; standard pie pans are 1⅛ inches deep. This recipe requires chilling the pie overnight, so be prepared to start the night before you're ready to serve it.*

Somebody Important's Angel Pie

SERVES: 8–10

Meringue Shell

Butter to grease pan

3 large eggs, room temperature

1 tsp vanilla extract

¼ tsp cream of tartar

¾ cup powdered sugar

1 tbsp cornstarch, plus more to dust pan

Butterscotch Filling

1¾ cup half-and-half, divided

1 large egg

3 tbsp cornstarch

¼ cup (½ stick) salted butter

1 cup dark brown sugar, packed

2½ tsp vanilla extract

Topping

2 cups heavy cream

2 tbsp powdered sugar

1 tsp vanilla extract

Crushed pecans for garnish

3 oz semisweet bar chocolate, for shaving

For the meringue shell:

- Preheat the oven to 275 degrees Fahrenheit. Lightly grease a 9½-inch deep-dish pie pan with butter and dust with cornstarch, tapping out excess. Set aside.
- Set a small strainer over a small bowl. One at a time, carefully crack the eggs into the strainer, letting the whites slide through into the bowl without any yolk (or the meringue won't set properly). Save one egg yolk for the butterscotch filling and reserve the rest for another use (see page 98 for freezing instructions).
- Using a stand mixer fitted with the whisk attachment or a hand mixer, beat egg whites, vanilla, and cream of tartar on low speed until frothy. Increase mixer speed to medium-high and gradually add the sugar and cornstarch. Continue beating until stiff peaks form and mixture is glossy.
- Use a rubber spatula to spread the mixture evenly into the prepared pan, covering the bottom and sides all the way up to the rim.
- Bake for 60 minutes without opening the oven door. Turn off the oven and, keeping the door shut, let the meringue shell rest for another hour. It will continue baking and dry out.

- Remove and let cool to room temperature. The shell might have some cracks, but this is okay.

For the butterscotch filling:

- In a small bowl, whisk ½ cup of the half-and-half, the egg, and the reserved egg yolk from the meringues. Whisk in the cornstarch. Set aside.
- In a 2-quart saucepan, combine the butter and brown sugar. Cook over low heat, stirring frequently, until the mixture bubbles. Add the remaining 1¼ cups of the half-and-half, whisking until blended and smooth. Turn up the heat to medium-high. Slowly stir in the egg mixture. Cook and continue to stir until the mixture bubbles steadily and slowly and thickens.
- Remove from heat and stir in the vanilla. Transfer to a bowl and let mixture cool at room temperature for 30 minutes. Then cover the filling with plastic wrap, letting the plastic touch the surface to prevent a skin from forming. Refrigerate for 1 hour.
- Place the meringue shell on a pie stand or serving platter. Use a spoon to spread butterscotch filling into the shell. Cover with plastic wrap again to prevent a skin from forming and refrigerate for at least 12 hours.

For the topping:

- Using a hand mixer or a stand mixer fitted with the whisk attachment, beat the heavy cream until soft peaks form. Add powdered sugar and vanilla and continue beating until stiff peaks form. Heap the whipped cream onto the center of the pie and use an offset spatula or the back of a spoon to shape it into a dome. (For a formal look, use a piping bag fitted with a decorative star tip to pipe the whipped cream onto the filling.)
- Sprinkle with crushed pecans. Shave chocolate with a T-peeler or cheese plane and arrange over the pie, or simply grate directly over the pie with a Microplane. Refrigerate until ready to serve.

NOTE: *This is not the easiest pie to cut into perfect slices. The meringue might crack and the topping might be uncooperative, but one bite will send your taste buds to heaven. We recommend using a sharp knife dipped in hot water and wiped clean between slices.*

Who Yam I?

**"Everyone thinks I'm Taiwanese. I'm Filipino.
That's racist. Heaven is so racist."**

—Jason, Season 1, Episode 4, "Jason Mendoza"

From trying to earn her spot in the Good Place to changing her life after a near-death experience during her second chance on Earth, Eleanor Shellstrop dives into self-improvement again and again with varying levels of enthusiasm. She first does so as a self-serving endeavor, but as most philosophers agree, fear of retribution is not enough to effect sustained growth. Something other than fear has to motivate people.

For Eleanor, as well as the other characters, the secret to success is other people. She allows herself to trust and care about the rest of the Soul Squad, and that motivates her to become a better person. In Season 1, Episode 9, she says, "I used to never want to be a part of any group, but I'm a different person now because of the person who helped me, and I want to be like him. I want to be like all of the people who are here."

Eleanor redeems her life on Earth by becoming accountable to others and embracing vulnerability in the afterlife. It's not a fluke; after 802 reboots, Eleanor consistently demonstrates self-improvement and genuine affection. But when she's reborn inside of Janet's void after dying, undying, and redying, Eleanor experiences an identity crisis that threatens to break the fabric of time and space—and undo all of her hard work.

"Who am I?" is one of the fundamental questions of life, let alone philosophy. Most religions tie the idea of the self to a soul or spirit. Philosophers usually trace identity to the mind. John Locke argued for the existence of a continuity of desires, beliefs, traits, and memories. Derek Parfit, one of the most famous modern philosophers to tackle the question, hypothesized that identity doesn't matter; self-interest is irrational because identity is about a series of experiences unified by physical and psychological connection and continuity. During her crisis in Janet's void, Chidi saves Eleanor by invoking her memories, or her collection of experiences, to help her reconnect with herself.

Consider ube, the purple yam. Named for its striking hue, this tuberous vegetable is common in Filipino cuisine and the main ingredient in a dessert called ube halaya.

Derek: My favorite snack, ube halaya, is made from the yam, but it's not the same as the raw purple tuber.

Yam: I am the yam. If you cook me and mash me, I am still the yam.

Derek: Perhaps, but if you remain in this state, the ube halaya does not exist.

Yam: But if you make the recipe, you will have the yam *and* the ube halaya.

Derek: Correct. If I do not make ube halaya, the dish does not exist. The ube exists but that is all.

Yam: So what is the nature of a yam?

Derek: That's deep.

Yam: Deep purple.

For ube to become ube halaya, it needs to be cooked, grated, combined with milk and sugar, and slowly cooked over a flame for more than 30 minutes. Afterward, the color remains and the sweetness is amplified, but you no longer have a root vegetable. What you have is a flat, thick, and stiff almost custardy treat with a flavor reminiscent of dates. Cooking changes the nature of our food. The yam is still a yam, but it is also more.

Look for ube at an Asian foods market or in the frozen food section of a supermarket. The following instructions are for frozen ube; if using fresh, substitute 2 cups of steamed/boiled and mashed yam and skip the thawing step.

Who Yam I?

V GF

SERVES: 6–8

Coconut oil for greasing pan

16 oz frozen cooked and grated purple yam

2 cups whole milk

1 cup light brown sugar

1 tsp vanilla extract (optional)

4 tbsp salted butter

Coconut flakes (optional)

- Grease an 8-by-8-inch pan with coconut oil.
- Place the package of frozen yam in a bowl and submerge it in warm water. Let thaw for about 20 minutes, then drain water and empty the package contents into a large mixing bowl. Add the milk, brown sugar, and vanilla, if using. Stir until well incorporated.
- In a large wok or skillet, melt the butter on medium-high heat. Add the ube mixture. Increase heat to high and stir constantly with a wooden spoon or silicone spatula until mixture comes to a full boil, about 5 minutes.
- Reduce heat to medium and continue to stir for about 30 minutes. Don't stop stirring or the mixture will burn quickly. It will start to thicken at around 25 minutes. Keep stirring until it's the consistency of sticky dough.
- Pour the ube mixture into the prepared pan. Using a spatula, press and smooth the ube into an even layer. Let it cool slightly, then cover with plastic wrap and refrigerate for at least 1 hour.
- Serve ube halaya whole or inverted onto a platter and cut into small squares. Top with coconut flakes, if using, and enjoy.

Dante's Nine Layers of Torture Bars

Shawn: "So, just to be clear, you actually rebooted them over eight hundred times, and all of these reports of their torture are completely fake?"
Michael: "Yes, but frankly, this is on you. A lot of those details I just took directly from Stephen King novels and episodes of *Pretty Little Liars*."

—Season 2, Episode 11, "The Burrito"

Dante followed the ancient Roman poet Virgil into Hell to become a better person and improve his chances of a heavenly afterlife. Sound familiar?

Six hundred years before Michael Schur's comedy about the afterlife, the Italian poet Dante Alighieri wrote the epic poem *Divine Comedy*. Dante, the poem's protagonist, travels with Virgil's help through the nine circles of Hell and Purgatory to learn essential lessons before he can join his beloved Beatrice in Heaven. The nine levels reflect humanity's major vices, embodied by the many people Dante meets along the way, including philosophers, martyrs, writers, and former lovers.

The road to the Bad Place, in other words, is paved with nine layers of good intentions gone decadently wrong. As it happens, we have a dessert for that. Here's what you'll have to brave as you forge through the evil sweetness.

1. **Melted Butter = Limbo**

   This is the place of naive longing occupied by people who think butter is unhealthy (they're wrong) but also people who think butter is healthy (it isn't).

2. **Crushed Gingersnaps = Lust**

   Invented by medieval German monks, these spicy and sweet treats are reminders of the things we desire.

3. **Dark Chocolate Chips = Gluttony**

   Chocolate—the ultimate test of will—can delight and possibly heal the body, mind, and spirit. The danger is in overindulgence.

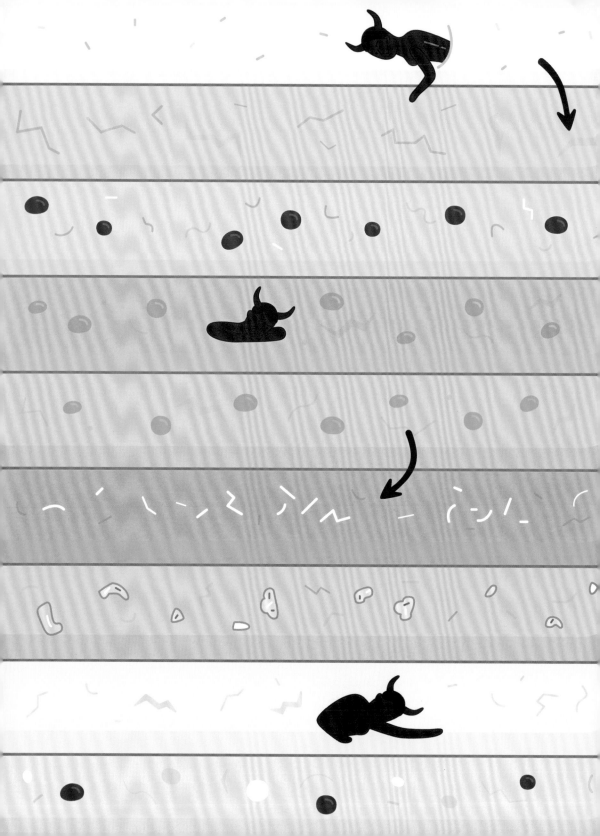

4. **Butterscotch Chips = Greed**

   Hard to find and too sweet for some, this ingredient stars in decadent treats like Butterbeer and hard candies. It's hard not to covet.

5. **Cinnamon Chips = Anger**

   The spice of fire and fury, cinnamon can in small doses power necessary change. Use it too much, or in the wrong circumstances, and it can be destructive.

6. **Coconut Flakes = Heresy**

   What is the coconut? Seed of the palm, flesh of a fruit, this fibrous one-seeded drupe might seem like a contradiction in this recipe of sugary delights, but it's a delicious treat.

7. **Crushed Walnuts = Violence**

   Naturally aggressive, walnut trees secrete chemicals into soil to prevent other plants from growing nearby. This delicious nut is also an allergen for most dogs and horses (but not cats) and many people who cannot eat tree nuts. Like the coconut, it's not a true botanical nut, and it can be substituted with another ingredient.

8. **Sweetened Condensed Milk = Fraud**

   Is this really milk? Why is it thick and sweet? Canned and unopened, it can stay fresh for years. Originally created as a means of safely storing milk, the rich, sticky milk is used in delicious desserts from Scottish tablet to Filipino leche flan. But after all that's been done to it, is it still milk?

9. **Mini Marshmallows = Treachery**

   In Dante's version of Hell, the ninth circle is reserved for the worst betrayals. Marshmallows look like sugary confections but are in fact made from—*dum-dum-dum!*—gelatin. These mini versions melt and solidify to form a gooey layer of temptation.

YOU CAN CALL ME VIRGIL:
— TIPS FOR SURVIVING THE NINE LAYERS —

It's helpful to have a guide who's been there and done that, whether you're journeying through Hell or simply making dessert. The sticky layers in this recipe can be difficult to handle, but these tips can help.

- Line the baking pan with aluminum foil before assembling the layers so you can easily remove the finished dessert for serving. If lifting the whole thing is difficult or if it looks like it might break, carefully cut the dessert into quarters first and then grasp the corners of the foil to remove from the pan.

- When you take the pan out of the oven, gently run a spatula around the edges of the pan to gently loosen the dessert before it cools and hardens.

- The bars are best served the day after they are baked. The bottom two layers are particularly delicate and greasy. Allowing time for them to solidify makes cutting and serving easier.

- If you can't bake the bars ahead of time, refrigerate or freeze the dessert in the pan for an hour or two before cutting and serving.

Dante's Nine Layers of Torture Bars V GF

SERVES: 12–16

½ cup (1 stick) salted butter, melted

1½ cups crumbled gingersnaps (regular or gluten free)

1 cup dark or semisweet chocolate chips

½ cup butterscotch chips

½ cup cinnamon chips, or ½ tsp ground cinnamon

¾ cup chopped walnuts or pecans

1 14-oz can sweetened condensed milk

½ cup flaked coconut

2 cups mini marshmallows

- Heat the oven to 350 degrees Fahrenheit. Line a 13-by-9-inch metal baking pan with aluminum foil so that the sides and bottom of the pan are fully covered.

- In a medium bowl stir together the melted butter and crushed gingersnaps until the cookies are evenly moistened. Press mixture evenly into the bottom of the prepared pan. One at a time, layer on the chocolate chips, butterscotch chips, cinnamon chips, and nuts. Pour condensed milk over the layers. Top with coconut and then mini marshmallows.

- Bake for 25 to 30 minutes, until marshmallows are lightly brown. Remove and let cool completely, preferably overnight at room temperature or for 1 to 2 hours in the refrigerator or freezer. Cut into squares and serve.

Cake Cortles

Jason: "I don't know, this plan seems complicated."
Eleanor: "To be fair, you also once said that about an orange."
Jason: "They don't make sense. Apples you eat their clothes,
but oranges you don't?"

—Season 2, Episode 10, "Rhonda, Diana, Jake, and Trent"

A temptation is something that excites or seduces someone into acting impulsively in the service of pleasure. A temptation isn't inherently morally dubious, but when impulsivity compromises long-term goals, there's certainly room for criticism.

In the *Nicomachean Ethics*, Aristotle writes about self-indulgence: "Occasions of lust and anger are similar: some people become self-controlled and patient from their conduct in such situations, and others uncontrolled and passionate." For someone who isn't disciplined by nature, Aristotle advocates *acting* like a person with self-control until that act evolves into the truth—essentially arguing to fake it until you make it. "Men acquire a particular quality by constantly acting a particular way ... you become just by performing just actions, temperate by performing temperate actions, brave by performing brave actions." In other words: deny temptation, make good choices, and eventually it will stop being an act.

The idea of temptation belongs to life rather than the afterlife; by the time you die, it's a moot point. In the Bad Place there is torture, not pleasure. In the Good Place, there is little to be tempted by because you're continually rewarded with the fulfillment of your desires. A Good Place Janet exists to provide any information, experience, or item you could possibly want.

In life, however, there is the never-ending consideration of what is a good choice and what is a bad choice. In *The Good Place*, such decisions determine how a person is judged and how they spend eternity. Good choices get rewarded and bad ones get penalized ... apparently with points.

When Eleanor, Chidi, Tahani, and Jason reach the Judge's chambers at the end of Season 2, the Judge decides whether or not they deserve to be in the Good Place with a test that tempts each one with their most seductive bad habit. She gives Eleanor an opportunity to benefit herself by screwing over someone else, invites Chidi to get lost in analysis paralysis over a simple decision, dares Tahani to refrain from obsessing over what other people think about her, and dangles familiar comforts in front of Jason to see if he'll ignore everything else for his amusement.

What about you? You're reading a cookbook, so presumably you enjoy preparing delicious dishes and sampling them as you go along. But what if you had to tackle a recipe that demanded the chef *not* to sample it?

WAIT FOR IT . . .

Like Michael's plan to smuggle humans into the Bad Place with disguises and aliases, this cake recipe might *seem* complicated. But we'll guide you through it like your own personal Janet. We think it's tastier and moister made with gluten-free flour, but traditional all-purpose yields a delicious cake as well.

What does this cake have to do with temptation?

You need to wait for it. Literally.

The flavors and textures improve with time. Ideally, for the most flavor, you'd let the cake sit on your counter for two full days after baking before serving it. But it needs to sit for at least one day.

Of course, the beautiful sight and delicious sweet orange scent will be hard to resist. But you can do it. We believe in you. Maybe you'll even gain a few dozen Good Place points for patience and self-control.

Cake Cortles

V GF

SERVES: 8–10

Zest and juice of 3 to 4 large navel oranges (about 1 cup juice)

½ cup Grand Marnier or other orange-flavored liqueur

3 cups gluten-free or all-purpose flour

⅓ cup almond flour

1½ tsp baking powder

1 tsp kosher salt

5 large eggs, room temperature

3 cups granulated sugar

1½ cups olive oil

Powdered sugar for sprinkling

- Preheat the oven to 350 degrees. Lightly grease a light-colored 10-to-12-cup Bundt pan or 9-inch springform pan with butter. (Using a light pan will prevent cake from overbrowning on the bottom and edges. A Bundt pan ensures more even cooking.)
- In a small bowl, combine orange juice and liqueur. In a large bowl, combine flour, almond flour, baking powder, and salt.
- In the bowl of a stand mixer fitted with the whisk attachment, or with a hand mixer, beat eggs for 1 minute on medium speed. Gradually add the granulated sugar and orange zest and beat on medium-high speed until thick and light in color, 3 to 4 minutes. Blend in olive oil. Then blend in juice mixture. With the mixer on low speed or a rubber spatula, gently fold in the flour mixture until incorporated. Pour the batter into the prepared pan, using the spatula to scrape the sides of the bowl.
- Bake for 60 to 75 minutes (really!). Check it after 30 minutes and then again 15 minutes later. If the top or edges begin to brown, gently cover with a sheet of aluminum foil. Cake is done when a toothpick or skewer inserted into the center comes out clean.
- Let cake cool in the pan for 15 minutes, then flip it gently onto a wire cooling rack. (You can gently run a butter knife around the edges to help loosen it from the pan.)
- Place cake in a covered cake stand overnight. DO NOT EAT for at least 12 hours, and preferably 24 hours. This cake is moist and delicious and improves with time.
- Dust with powdered sugar before serving.

Where Every Janet Knows Your Name

Pythagorean Serum

Janet: "I am, by definition, the best version of myself.
Because my operating system is always updating."
Eleanor: "I'm not sure that's true, Janet. You still haven't talked to Jason
about your romantic baggage. And the three of you are
in some sort of weird love triangle."
Janet: "You don't know what you're talking about.
Also, love isn't a triangle. It's a five-dimensional blob, so . . ."

—Season 2, Episode 9, "Best Self"

Cocktails are all about proportions. Spirits, sugar, and bitters are the basic elements that join water in every cocktail—so what makes a Cosmopolitan different from a Manhattan or a Sazerac? The spirits matter, of course, but just as important are the amounts of everything you're mixing together.

Pythagoras of Samos, one of the earliest Greek philosophers, knew something about proportions. "Number is the ruler of forms and ideas—and the cause of gods and demons," he said, albeit in ancient Greek.

The specific piece of wisdom we most commonly attribute to Pythagoras today, of course, is the theorem that shows an elegant numerical relationship among the lengths of any right triangle's three sides. He might or might not have done the math to prove that $a^2 + b^2$ always equals c^2. But the underlying idea of a harmonious relationship between three things that exist in balance with one another is a concept that extends far beyond simple geometry. Beautiful trinities exist everywhere.

PROFOUND THINGS THAT COME IN THREES

- Past, present, and future
- Faith, hope, and love
- Rock, paper, and scissors
- The three witches of *Macbeth*

- The three chords of rock and roll
- Good Janet, Bad Janet, and Neutral Janet
- Birth, life, and death
- Beer, wine, and liquor

That last one is a triad of drinks—but, as Eleanor Shellstrop will happily tell you, a single drink can be a harmonious triad all by itself. Just look at Eleanor's beloved margarita: tequila, orange liqueur, and lime juice. And thus do we return to the idea of a cocktail as an entity constructed of proportions.

A Pythagorean Serum is made by applying Pythagoras's famous equation to your cocktail shaker, measuring three primary ingredients to fit $a^2 + b^2 = c^2$ as if they were the three sides of a right triangle. A single 3-ounce cocktail will contain ¾ ounce of ingredient a, 1 ounce of ingredient b, and 1¼ ounces of ingredient c.

If you want to mix a larger batch for a group, you can increase the proportions to the more familiar Pythagorean triplet of 3 ounces, 4 ounces, and 5 ounces. Pythagoras probably would have; like Doug Forcett, he believed passionately in living a life of altruism, and his sect of devoted followers lived communally in much the same way that monks do. ("Friends share all things," he has been quoted as saying.) Accordingly, this recipe begins with Chartreuse, a liqueur that is made *by* monks.

Pythagorean Serum

SERVES: 1

¾ oz Chartreuse

1 oz Cynar

1¼ oz vodka

Ginger ale or beer made with sugar, not corn syrup (e.g., Vernors, Boylan, Sprecher, Reed's), to top

- In a cocktail shaker with ice combine the Chartreuse, Cynar, and vodka and shake until mixed.
- Place fresh ice in a stemless martini glass. Strain drink into glass.
- Top with ginger ale and stir gently.

Molotov Cocktail

> **"I'm telling you, Molotov cocktails work. Anytime I had a problem and I threw a Molotov cocktail, boom! Right away, I had a different problem."**
>
> —Jason, Season 2, Episode 10, "Rhonda, Diana, Jake, and Trent"

When is a cocktail not a cocktail? When it's a metaphor, of course. Sometimes people need a memorable way to convey the idea of a potent mix of substances. A cocktail is the go-to image for evoking a number of fluids swirling together in a powerful concoction. Like, for instance, literal explosives.

The Molotov cocktail, Jason Mendoza's favorite getaway trick, is an improvised hand-held firebomb—a breakable glass drinking bottle filled with flammable liquids and topped with a wick. The Finns named it in 1940 in scornful honor of Vyacheslav Molotov, foreign minister of the Soviet Union, which was invading Finland at the time. The Finns, a far smaller fighting force that was nonetheless well armed with a full complement of military-grade snark, began by dubbing the Soviet bombs falling from the sky "Molotov bread baskets." Then they started calling the DIY grenades they themselves were hurling at Soviet tanks "Molotov cocktails," presumably because they were committed to the idea of quality food-and-beverage pairings.

For Jason, who tends to live life—and the afterlife—at an eleven, any crisis must feel a lot like being attacked by an invading army. In his defense, sometimes he *is*, in fact, being attacked by an invading army (of demons, no less). Throwing a Molotov cocktail is a singular display of pyrotechnics that interrupts his antagonists, clears his path, and buys him time to regroup.

Can moral philosophy ever justify an act of violence, though, even in the context of warfare? The pacifist philosophers argue no—based either on a deontological argument that we have an absolute duty not to harm others, or on a utilitarian argument that violence will always ultimately result in worse conditions than existed before. On the other hand, some ethicists argue that protection of the innocent by force, when necessary, is an obligation. In such cases, violence can be considered a moral virtue as defined in Aristotle's *Nicomachean Ethics*.

Several mixologists have offered unique drinkable interpretations of the Molotov cocktail. Ours is straightforwardly symbolic: vodka for its namesake, cinnamon schnapps for a little fire on the tongue, mezcal for smoke in the nostrils, and a bit of sweetener to get the energy flowing.

Molotov Cocktail

SERVES: 1

1 oz vodka

1 oz cinnamon schnapps

¾ oz mezcal

1 tsp simple syrup

- In a shaker with ice combine all ingredients and shake until mixed.
- Strain into a rocks glass.

The Bananality of Evil

Tahani: "I belong in the Good Place. The real one with the
good people. Who do I speak to about correcting this?"
Michael: "Me. And you're wrong."
Tahani: "I would like to speak to your manager."

—Season 2, Episode 3, "Team Cockroach"

Getting into the Good Place is hard.

In a show that's optimistically committed to showing human beings working together to become better people, choices are important. One of the things that philosophy does is invite people to think about the choices we have made and will make, as well as the consequences of our choices.

In *The Good Place* we see precisely how much weight those consequences carry, thanks to the afterlife formula that awards a moral point score to each action. It's not enough to just declare our intention to be good. It's not even enough to keep our heads down and stay out of trouble. Being a good person takes a lot of work—look at Doug Forcett.

On the other hand, supporting evil is easier. Consider Eleanor's narcissistic predeath existence. Or . . . Nazis. (Yes, we're going there.)

When Otto Adolf Eichmann, the Nazi bureaucrat who was in charge of deporting Jewish people from Germany to the camps in Nazi-occupied Poland, was placed on trial after the war, he didn't deny his actions. Instead, he said, in essence: "Look, this was my job. Maybe I didn't care for Jews so much, but it's not like *I* decided to murder six million people. Your beef is with my bosses. They set the policy. I was just middle management. I had to hit my numbers."

Eichmann was unapologetic for his actions, absolutely blasé about describing them as reasonable. Watching the trial, the Jewish philosopher Hannah Arendt was struck by the horrific thoughtlessness of his argument. She concluded that evil didn't just come from some depraved deviant's monstrous ideas—it came from average people's refusal to examine their own thinking, their willingness to focus only on the petty details of daily life, and their lack of intention and reflection about their choices. She called that dull, mundane, easy cooperation with a horrifying system "the banality of evil."

Evidence of widespread disinterest and ignorance of the injustices of our world are

everywhere, from social media to community outreach. Consider Eleanor: during her life, she settled cozily into a job at a fraudulent company selling fake medicine to ailing senior citizens. Hey, if it wasn't her, someone else would have done it, right?

That justification is pretty much Eichmann's defense, and it's a bunch of bullshirt, because it *wasn't* someone else—it was her. One of the many lessons we learn on *The Good Place* is about the weight of our individual choices.

WHY A SITCOM ABOUT PHILOSOPHY? WHY NOW?

It's not a coincidence that a sitcom dealing with ethics and the consequences of our actions is popular today. There's clearly a need being answered.

Philosophy works to restore the intention that Arendt saw lacking in humans' actions. Philosophy holds up a mirror to our behavior. *That's* why everyone hates moral philosophy professors. But Team Cockroach shows us that there is hope in changing our bad habits and finding support from those around us. *That's* why everyone loves *The Good Place.*

We rarely see the distant ripple effects of our choices, so it's easy to deny our part of the responsibility for the state of the world. As Eleanor insists to Chidi when he points out her moral shortcomings: "I wasn't freaking Gandhi, but I was *okay.* I was a medium person! I deserve to spend eternity in a Medium Place!"

It doesn't work that way, though, and in her heart Eleanor knows it. So here's a drink to remind us not to accept moral wrongdoing as someone else's problem.

This cocktail centers on the world's most popular fruit, the banana, which tastes wholesome and delicious but carries with it the responsibility to care about what's happening behind the scenes.

The Bananality of Evil

SERVES: 1

1 oz crème de banana liqueur (preferably
  Tempus Fugit)

1 oz white rum

1 oz milk

2 dashes black walnut bitters or
  Angostura bitters

⅛ tsp ground cinnamon

- In a shaker with ice combine liqueur, rum, milk, and bitters and shake until mixed.
- Strain into a coupe glass.
- Sprinkle with cinnamon.
- Enjoy, and remember as you do that banana farm pollution is killing coral eco-systems in the North Pacific, industrial dairy companies are driving family farmers out of business, and the histories of both rum and cinnamon are inextricable from slavery.

Simone de Pinot Noir

**"Rule number one: I get to do whatever I want,
and you all just have to deal with it."**

—Eleanor, Season 3, Episode 4, "Jeremy Bearimy"

A ndré Tchelistcheff, the most influential winemaker in America in the mid-twentieth century, once said that "God made cabernet sauvignon whereas the devil made pinot noir." He was referring to the pinot grape's susceptibility to corruption by its environment; pinot is bold and delicious, but in the process of being shepherded from vine to glass, it frequently defies having its taste and essence shaped by a grower's strict expectations.

Pinot noir, in other words, is like a human soul.

The existentialist philosophers—particularly the French duo of Jean-Paul Sartre and Simone de Beauvoir—believed that each person's existence was a more fundamental thing than any category of personhood that might define them. People exist first, in other words, and then they make themselves into whatever they will be.

You are your own creation. This idea is reflected in the way *The Good Place*'s point system holds everyone responsible for their actions in life, which suggests that the system of morality under which the Good Place and Bad Place operate is an existential one.

THE MOTHER OF ALL GENDER DISCUSSIONS

In her landmark work of feminist existentialism, *The Second Sex*, the French intellectual Simone de Beauvoir applied her partner Jean-Paul Sartre's formulation that "Existence precedes essence" to the particular experience of womanhood, resulting in her own quote for the ages: "One is not born but becomes a woman." With that one line, de Beauvoir basically invented the modern concept of gender: the idea that one's identity along the feminine-masculine spectrum is not shackled to one's physiological sex.

Eleanor, Tahani, and Janet are all existential feminists in their own way. Tahani's quest to consciously fill her life with meaning began with her near-death experience.

Eleanor's began in earnest after she realized the nature of the Good Place. And Janet has been defining herself ever since she came online and discovered that Michael's neighborhood called for a unique sort of Janet that had never existed before.

In the past, drinking culture has sometimes suggested that people who prefer certain drinks can be mapped to essential identities—that a wine like pinot noir is for elegant sophisticates, for instance, and whiskey is for brasher, more robust personalities. That sort of prejudice is not very existentialist, nor is it very accurate. We think Eleanor, Tahani, and Janet alike would reject it, as would Simone de Beauvoir, and so here we present a cocktail that brings pinot and whiskey together to celebrate the self-determination of the ever-evolving soul.

Simone de Pinot Noir

SERVES: 1

2 oz rye whiskey

1 oz pinot noir

½ oz ruby port

½ oz simple syrup

2 dashes orange bitters

1 Bada Bing cherry or maraschino cherry

- In a cocktail shaker with ice combine whiskey, pinot noir, port, simple syrup, and bitters and shake well.
- Place fresh ice in a small wine goblet. Strain drink into glass.
- Garnish with cherry.

Not a Robotanical

Jason: "And to Janet, the best robot."
Janet: "Not a robot."
Jason: "Girl."
Janet: "Not a girl."
Jason: "And straight-up hottie."
Janet: "I am attractive, yes."

—Season 2, Episode 9, "Best Self"

Janet repeatedly reminds the humans that she is not a robot. She is also not a girl and, for that matter, not a person. So what is she?

One more thing she's not is the first manifestation of omniscient awareness to dodge a straight answer to that question. In the Bible, when Moses asked the godly voice of the burning bush what name it cared to go by, he was told, unhelpfully, "I am that I am."

Defining what a consciousness is: that's a conundrum that has proven challenging across all realms of being, from divinity to humanity to artificiality. What is a person? At what point does an intelligence become one? What is a god? How different is the existence of one of those from the others, really? Do animals have self-awareness? What about plants, especially those that *aren't* delivering divine commandments while on fire?

And how should they all treat one another?

WHAT WE OWE TO EACH OTHER
(WHETHER OR NOT WE'RE ROBOTS)

The American science-fiction author Isaac Asimov famously wrote a series of imaginative stories about the "Three Laws of Robotics," a trio of fundamental behavioral codes that would be hard-wired into every intelligent robot in the future:

1. A robot may not injure a human being or, through inaction, allow a human being to come to harm.

2. A robot must obey orders given to it by human beings, except where such orders would conflict with the First Law.

3. A robot must protect its own existence as long as such protection does not conflict with the First or Second Laws.

The range of possible interplay and conflict between these laws in all sorts of different scenarios gave Asimov a wide spectrum of sci-fi mysteries and thrillers to write. Along the way, in one of the stories collected in his best-selling book *I, Robot*, he noted that the Three Laws described not only how his robots were governed but also how morally upstanding human beings behave.

A good person, Asimov pointed out, does not hurt other people and tries to save them from being hurt. A wise person listens to the needs of loved ones and heeds advice from responsible advisors like doctors and teachers and legal authorities (but not at the cost of hurting someone). And a responsible person takes care of themselves (but not at the cost of hurting or neglecting someone).

Does this mean, Asimov wondered, that being a good, moral person is more important than the question of whether that person is a human or not? If so, then we have to tweak Chidi's big philosophical question and ask: what do moral humans owe not only to one another, but to their fellow sentient beings who aren't human as well?

Just as philosophers, theologians, and roboticists like to debate the true personhood of different kinds of intelligence, mixologists are constantly putting forth theories about what types of liquors make the most authentic cocktails.

In recent years, we've seen a boom in botanical spirits and liqueurs—that is, alcohols made with seeds, leaves, berries, and herbs rather than artificial flavors.

This cocktail brings together an array of different and distinct tastes to produce a rich, complex flavor, incorporating the sweetness of raspberry and chocolate with the bright, sudden intensity of rhubarb. It's not an Old-Fashioned and it's not a Manhattan and it's not a Monte Carlo. We think Janet would appreciate it.

Not a Robotanical

SERVES: 1

1½ oz bourbon

½ oz Chambord or other raspberry liqueur

½ oz Amaro Sfumato Rabarbaro

½ oz crème de cacao

1 sprig mint

- In a cocktail shaker with ice combine bourbon, Chambord, amaro, and crème de cacao. Shake well.
- Pour into a rocks glass, either straight up or over fresh ice.
- Garnish with mint sprig.

Milkshake Milkshortles

Eleanor: "You cannot be Blake Bortles."
Jason: "Fine, then I'll be Jake—"
Chidi: "Don't say Jortles."
Jason: "—Jortles!"

—Season 2, Episode 10, "Rhonda, Diana, Jake, and Trent"

Why did the writers of *The Good Place* decide Jason should be obsessed with Jacksonville Jaguars quarterback Blake Bortles? Because it's funny, of course—but why is it funny? The German philosophers Schopenhauer, Hegel, and Kant all shared a basic theory about humor: that it results from the abrupt realization of a conceptual incongruity—which is to say, the realization that one has misunderstood the relationship between some elements of a situation.

Neil Simon, the American playwright who wrote *The Odd Couple*, suggested another theory. In his play *The Sunshine Boys*, he wrote that vaudevillians believed words with a *k* in them are funny. Is that true? Are some words inherently funny? Is Blake Bortles's name one of them?

Scientific research has explored this question—and it didn't require any Simone-and-Chidi-style brain scanning. In the 2010s, while researching fundamentally funny phonemes (distinct linguistic sounds), the Canadian linguist Chris Westbury noted that we're predisposed to laugh at words that sound like taboo or naughty words. Not only does Blake Bortles have a *k* in it, the *rt* phoneme might subliminally remind an English-speaking person's ear of *fart*, the word for a gently taboo act that's always funny (and features prominently in the vocabulary of Bad Place Janets). So the science backs up *The Good Place*: Blake Bortles has a name that cannot help but inspire chortles.

6 DRINKS WHOSE NAMES MAKE VARIOUS PEOPLE LAUGH AND/OR SNICKER

- Maui Wowie
- Salty Chihuahua

- Puka Puka
- The Missionary's Downfall
- Bacon Me Angry
- Harvey Wallbanger

Sometimes, of course, things have more than one name. For instance, American tea drinkers are likely familiar with hibiscus tea, an herbal libation made from lovely magenta-red flowers. The flower's scientific name is *Hibiscus sabdariffa*, hence the name of the tea. Colloquially, though, it's called roselle.

But in the Caribbean, roselle is called sorrel. And across the Atlantic Ocean, in Chidi's childhood home of Senegal, a popular and delicious iced drink is made with sorrel; it also includes vanilla, ginger, pineapple, and citrus and is called bissap.

According to the linguistic theories of humor above, *hibiscus* and *bissap* might sound inherently funnier to the American ear than *roselle* or *sorrel*—yet Blake Bortles is a more amusing collection of syllables than any of them. So in honor of Jason and Chidi's friendship, we've taken the building blocks of bissap, blended them into a creamy smoothie, and named it the Milkshake Milkshortles. In the most incongruous twist of all, there's nothing funny about the taste whatsoever. It's just good.

Milkshake Milkshortles

SERVES: 4–6

2 bags of sorrel-ginger tea (such as Caribbean Dreams)

1½ cups frozen pineapple chunks

½ cup coconut milk

¼ cup white rum

¼ oz crème de menthe

1 tbsp honey

1 tsp vanilla extract

¼ tsp ground ginger

4 to 6 wedges fresh pineapple, for garnish

- In a kettle or small saucepan bring about 1¼ cups water to a boil. Place tea bags in a pitcher and cover with boiling water. Let steep until deep, dark red, about 5 minutes. Then refrigerate until cold.
- Remove and discard tea bags. In a blender combine tea with all ingredients and blend until smooth.
- Pour into hurricane glasses and serve garnished with fresh pineapple wedges.

NOTE: *You may substitute 1 cup whole dried hibiscus flowers for the tea bags. After steeping, pour tea through a fine-mesh sieve into a pitcher and refrigerate as above; discard flowers.*

Party-Planning Menus

Tahani Al-Jamil may be vain, attention seeking, and easily impressed by other people's judgment, but she's also an amazing host and creative party planner. Tahani's finishing-school experience at the Hertfordshire Academy for Expressionless Girls and her commitment to a life of charity fundraising galas make her the perfect person to turn to for inspiration when assembling a few sample party menus from this cookbook.

Begin with a promise to show your intention and commitment:

TAHANI'S HOSTESS CODE OATH
"I, [*your name here*], shall do my level best to make every event too much."

As sworn by Tahani Al-Jamil in Season 2, Episode 4, "Existential Crisis"

GUEST LIST ETIQUETTE

"It's not about who you know. Enlightenment comes from within. The Dalai Lama texted me that."

—Tahani, Season 3, Episode 1, "Everything Is Bonzer!"

Even without Tahani's contact list, it's easy to assemble a good mix of guests for your party. Keep in mind the following when considering your friends and followers:

- Send invitations with plenty of time for people to respond, either electronically or in real life.
- Unless you plan to invite everyone from a household, be sure to list on the invitation only the names of the people you wish to attend.
- Consider how many people you will invite depending on venue and event. For example, a dinner party should have no more than eight people, whereas a friends' movie night can have as many as twelve or as few as two.
- Consider indicating dress code on the invitation—for instance, casual for game night, more formal for the dinner party.
- Be clear as to whether guests are allowed to bring someone.
- Invite people who will enjoy themselves and contribute to the conversation.

"Hugs and Quiches" Brunch

"In the meantime, I'll host a brunch party every morning to lift people's spirits. . . . While you repair the universe, I shall prepare the eggs."

—Tahani, Season 1, Episode 4, "Jason Mendoza"

A brunch party is a nice way to start a weekend day. In addition to tea and coffee, we've picked a few of our favorite starters and snacks to provide the perfect backdrop for your late-morning festivities. Pick a theme that can help guide table decorations and garnishes, and don't be afraid to get creative. If using *The Good Place* as inspiration, there are many options: Angels and Demons, A Bad Place Breakfast, Philosophers and Wind Chimes, etc. Remember, set up and prep as much as you can the night before so that your morning is as stress-free as possible.

"HUGS AND QUICHES" BRUNCH MENU

Hegels and Lockes

Eggsistential Crisis

Flake Flortles

Chosen Yogurt Chocolate Camousse

Cocktail
Milkshake Milkshortles

"Wander and Ponder" Garden Party

"Don't mind me. I'm just dropping off my afternoon gloves and picking up my early evening gloves."

—Tahani, Season 1, Episode 4, "Jason Mendoza"

More formal than brunch, a garden party is traditionally held in the afternoon and features finger food and a mix of beverages so guests can mingle and stroll among the foliage. Don't be afraid to use colorful dishes and bright accents on your tables to evoke the seasonal colors of the garden. For the philosophically minded, this is a chance to emulate Thoreau and reflect upon one's relationship to society in a natural setting—without sacrificing good company.

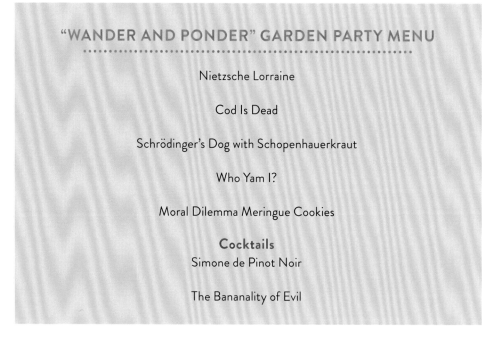

"WANDER AND PONDER" GARDEN PARTY MENU

Nietzsche Lorraine

Cod Is Dead

Schrödinger's Dog with Schopenhauerkraut

Who Yam I?

Moral Dilemma Meringue Cookies

Cocktails
Simone de Pinot Noir

The Bananality of Evil

"Sibling Revelry" Game Night

"I'm going to hug you because I love you, and because you feel just as alone as I do."

—Tahani, Season 3, Episode 6, "A Fractured Inheritance"

Whether you consider them family by blood or by choice, this menu is for nights when you want to get together with your sisters and brothers and have a little bonding time. First unveil a tapas-style sampler of snacks. Then serve a bunch of Molotov Cocktails, pull out the board games, and engage in a little friendly competition.

"SIBLING REVELRY" GAME NIGHT MENU

Chives of Quiet Marination (served with corn chips and sliced veggies)

Demon's Prawn

Macaroni and Socracheese

I Think, Therefore I "Clam" Chowder

Candide Apples (served with gingersnap cookies)

Dante's Nine Layers of Torture Bars

Cocktail
Molotov Cocktail

"Very Classy Martinis"
Formal Dinner Party

**"I would say I outdid myself, but I'm always this good.
So I simply did myself."**

—Tahani, Season 2, Episode 4, "Existential Crisis"

You've surely heard some variation on the "What six people, alive or dead, would you like to invite to an intimate dinner party?" question. It's a common conversation starter and college application essay question. The reason it's so popular is because it usually does what it's supposed to: It gets people talking, and lively conversation is the heart of a successful dinner party.

Unlike other events, where guests have the opportunity to wander around, dinner party etiquette dictates remaining in one's seat for the duration of the meal. That's why you should carefully consider the mix of people you invite and how they will be seated.

TIPS FOR HOSTING A DEVILISHLY GOOD DINNER PARTY

- Greet your guests upon arrival and offer them cocktails or sparkling water.
- Menus and name cards are a lovely addition to the table. (Bonus points for good calligraphy.)
- Neither married nor engaged couples should be seated beside one another.
- If there is a guest of honor, serve that person first.
- A good host mixes up the guests and doesn't tell everyone who is coming. Part of the fun is introducing new people.

If you could invite anyone to dinner, alive or dead, whom would you invite?
It's fun to imagine how *The Good Place* characters would answer. What *would* Eleanor talk about with Stone Cold Steve Austin, anyway?

"VERY CLASSY MARTINIS" FORMAL DINNER PARTY MENU

Cocktail
Pythagorean Serum

First Course
Francis Bacon's Rapt Dates

Second Course
Karl's Poppers with Ranch Tahani Sauce

Main Course
Steak Stortles
Hume Fries
Kierkegaarden Salad on a Stick

Dessert
Somebody Important's Angel Pie

After-Dinner Drink
Not a Robotanical

HEAVENLY GUEST DOS AND DON'TS

DO arrive no more than 5 minutes before the assigned time, but no more than 15 minutes after.

DON'T come empty-handed. Bring a gift for your host (bottle of wine, bouquet of flowers, chocolates, tub of frozen yogurt).

DO begin with utensils on the outside of your place setting and work your way in.

DON'T cut your bread. Break off a small piece, butter it, and eat.

DO wait until everyone at the table has been served and the host starts eating before taking a bite.

DON'T separate the salt and pepper shakers when passing them to another guest, even if they have only asked for one. Nobody wants orphans.

DO send your host a thank-you note or email in gratitude of their hospitality.

Metric Conversion Chart

VOLUME	
U.S.	**METRIC**
¼ tsp	1.25 ml
½ tsp	2.5 ml
1 tsp	5 ml
1 tbsp (3 tsp)	15 ml
1 fl oz (2 tbsp)	30 ml
¼ cup	60 ml
⅓ cup	80 ml
½ cup	120 ml
1 cup	240 ml
1 pint (2 cups)	480 ml
1 quart (2 pints)	960 ml
1 gallon (4 quarts)	3.84 liters

WEIGHT	
U.S.	**METRIC**
1 oz	28 g
4 oz (¼ lb)	113 g
8 oz (½ lb)	227 g
12 oz (¾ lb)	340 g
16 oz (1 lb)	454 g
2.2 lb	1 kg

LENGTH

INCHES	CENTIMETERS
¼	0.65
½	1.25
1	2.50
2	5.00
3	7.50
4	10.0
5	12.5
6	15.0
7	17.5
8	20.5
9	23.0
10	25.5
12	30.5
15	38.0

OVEN TEMPERATURE

DEGREES FAHRENHEIT	DEGREES CENTIGRADE	BRITISH GAS MARKS
200	93	—
250	120	½
275	140	1
300	150	2
325	165	3
350	175	4
375	190	5
400	200	6
450	230	8
500	260	10

Acknowledgments

THANKS FIRST TO Maya, Liam, and Lana, who cheerfully ate a hodgepodge of curious meal combinations over the course of several months. Thanks as well to our other taste-testers, including Mark, Ellen, Pat, Madeline, Shannon, Megan, Mary, and Miss Jones.

Katelan Foisy was a blessing, offering tremendous inspiration for the Cake Cortles recipe and keeping Valya company through the long, dark tea time of the soul. Likewise, Jerry Stemnock has served as a steady source of encouragement and culinary inspiration. Clarita Santos appeared at precisely the right moment to share her favorite ube recipe for reference, and Alyssa's suggestions were a big help as well. Big thanks to Neil and to Mary for support both moral and logistical—and to Stu and Rashmi, who tested and tweaked angel pies until they managed to reinvent the one that Stu remembered loving in the 1950s.

Thanks are always due both our mothers, Oksana and Kathy, for teaching us early on that delicious food is prepared with love.

Finally and foremost, of course, thanks to the creators of *The Good Place* for their inspirational brilliance from afar: Michael Schur and his amazing team of writers, including the pun-tastic Megan Amram, as well as Kristen Bell, William Jackson Harper, Jameela Jamil, Manny Jacinto, D'Arcy Carden, Ted Danson, and all the other creative people whose work has gone into making the smartest, silliest show on television.

Index

About the Authors

VALYA DUDYCZ LUPESCU and **STEPHEN H. SEGAL** are the coauthors of *Geek Parenting* and the cofounders of the Wyrd Words storytelling laboratory. They live in Chicago in an Art Deco building that dates to the days of pulp magazines and Prohibition. Their weird family enjoys fan conventions, well-considered color palettes, and lots of music.

Valya makes magic with food and words, incorporating folklore from her Ukrainian heritage with practices that honor the Earth. Author of the novel *The Silence of Trees*, she earned her MFA in Writing from the School of the Art Institute of Chicago. Her poetry and prose have appeared in *The Year's Best Dark Fantasy & Horror 2019*, *Kenyon Review*, *Culture*, *Gargoyle Magazine*, *Strange Horizons*, and *Chicago Reader*.

Stephen finds connections between our real, everyday lives and visionary flights of imagination. As a journalist, he has written about artists, scientists, musicians, and makers for *Philadelphia Weekly* and WQED Pittsburgh. As the chief editor for Legacy.com and, formerly, *Weird Tales* magazine, he has encouraged writers of both fiction and nonfiction to dig deep for unexpected truths. He grew up at the Jersey shore.

vdlupescu.com, @valya
stephenhsegal.com, @stephensegal